NEWSMAKERS

NEWSMAKERS

ARTIFICIAL INTELLIGENCE AND
THE FUTURE OF JOURNALISM

Francesco Marconi

Columbia University Press
New York

Columbia University Press
Publishers Since 1893
New York   Chichester, West Sussex
cup.columbia.edu
Copyright © 2020 Columbia University Press
All rights reserved

Library of Congress Cataloging-in-Publication Data

Names: Marconi, Francesco, author.
Title: Newsmakers : artificial intelligence and the future
   of journalism / Francesco Marconi.
Description: New York : Columbia University Press, 2020. | Includes
   bibliographical references and index.
Identifiers: LCCN 2019028576 (print) | LCCN 2019028577 (ebook) | ISBN
   9780231191364 (cloth) | ISBN 9780231191371 (paperback) | ISBN
   9780231549356 (ebook)
Subjects: LCSH: Journalism—Technological innovations. | Artificial
   intelligence.
Classification: LCC PN4784.T34 M35 2020 (print) | LCC PN4784.T34 (ebook)
   DDC 070.4/3—dc23
LC record available at https://lccn.loc.gov/2019028576
LC ebook record available at https://lccn.loc.gov/2019028577

Columbia University Press books are printed on
   permanent and durable acid-free paper.
Printed in the United States of America

Book design by Tammy Lian

For my parents and my wife.

CONTENTS

PREFACE

Recent advancements in technology have created a journalism landscape calling for faster news from more responsive newsrooms. In this environment, new processes and workflows are crucial if news organizations want the coming wave of artificial intelligence (AI) to help and not hinder journalism.

Artificial intelligence is here to stay, and it is likely to catapult humanity into a new era. In broad terms, AI refers to smart machines that learn from experience and perform humanlike tasks. More data combined with increased computing power will lead us to a new level of understanding about the world and our immediate surroundings.

Beyond changing society, artificial intelligence will alter how whole economies operate. Consulting firm PricewaterhouseCoopers estimates that by 2030 AI will potentially contribute $15.7 trillion to the global economy, with all regions across the globe expected to see a lift in their GDP as a direct result.[1]

Although some industries, such as communications, automotive production, and financial services, are already heavily investing in AI, the technology itself is still in a very early stage of development. The revolution propelled by smart machines will make some companies highly profitable, while putting others at risk of going out of business. Without proper knowledge and technical resources, no single organization can address the disruption ahead.

Now is the time to lay the foundations for successful change. For the news industry, that means rethinking how news is sourced and relayed to audiences. The result, AI-powered journalism, will require new levels of editorial and institutional oversight.

Smaller newsrooms, in particular, are at great risk of falling behind if they don't make artificial intelligence a key element in their transformation road map—and this will not require a big financial commitment, but it will require increased attention to training and culture change.

This book analyzes the challenges and opportunities of AI through detailed case studies, including newsrooms using algorithms to automatically produce stories, investigative reporters analyzing large sets of public data, and outlets dynamically determining the distribution of content across platforms.

The main message in *Newsmakers* is that AI can augment—not automate—the industry, allowing journalists to break more news more quickly while simultaneously freeing up their time for deeper analysis.

Whether you are a seasoned editor, a freelance journalist, or someone just out of J-school, my goal is to provide clarity and a practical road map for how AI can best serve news professionals. With technology costs lowering, smart software is now accessible to just about anyone. Soon, the majority of tools and processes across newsrooms will be powered by artificial intelligence.

In today's nascent model of twenty-first-century news media, editors are not only journalists but "information officers," who must be perpetually responsive to new audience needs, develop different story formats, and explore multiple distribution points, all while keeping an eye on emerging technologies that affect how news is produced and consumed. This is why journalists must adopt a more iterative form of their craft, one that leverages new technologies in order to respond in real time to the rapidly changing information needs of readers.

Iterative journalism is not simply about experimentation or being broadly open to new ideas. It's a responsive process informed by data that enables organizations to be driven by new technology, but not defined by it.

In this way and others, *Newsmakers* is not just another read on how to bring "innovation" or "emerging technology" into journalism. I should know. I've spent years implementing new processes in newsrooms: as an AI co-lead at the Associated Press and as the *Wall Street Journal*'s first research and development chief, leading a team of technologists, data scientists, and editors.

Unlike the distanced view you'll get from many manuals, what you are about to read is grounded in the field and practice of journalism. It outlines tested strategies, tools, and technologies through examples involving a not-so-distant-future version of a journalist I'm calling the Newsmaker, accompanied by best practices, failed experiments, and actionable approaches.

The information in this book explains how journalists at all seniority levels and newsrooms of all sizes (not just the big ones!) can integrate AI into their day-to-day work.

Newsmakers exist in every news organization. They are purpose-driven and eager to try new ideas; they look outside the newsroom for solutions and embrace collaboration. Most importantly, they are not afraid of failure. Each "failure" to them is a test, each test a step in the transformation of their newsrooms.

Using the Newsmaker as a model, this book cuts through the noise of news innovation clichés. Its tips are the byproducts of a process of trial and error, real applications, and media research. The discussion is conceptual rather than technical, and brevity (not intricacy) is the soul of it. This is not about what to do. It's about how to think—about journalism and the very future of the industry.

In three parts, this manual describes the problem—an industry in transition—and the solutions, including the artificial intelligence tools and technologies reinventing newsroom processes and finally, a workflow model for iterative journalism.

WHAT IS THIS BOOK ABOUT, ACCORDING TO AI?

A network graph of this book shows the terms mentioned with the highest frequency in proximity to one another. For example, every time the word "news" is mentioned, there's a high likelihood the terms "story," "consumers," and "organizations" also appear in the same sentence.

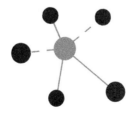

Most frequent words in the corpus: news (185); new (153); AI (139); newsmaker (122); data (114); journalism (112); story (79); journalists (77); content (72); technology (71); media (66); stories (63); newsroom (62); process (62).

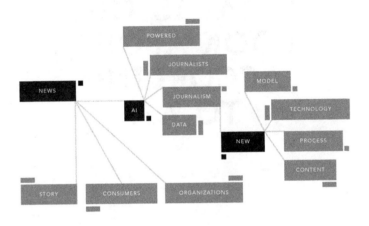

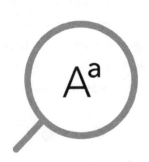

INTRODUCTION

TECHNOLOGY MOVES FASTER
THAN JOURNALISTIC STANDARDS

Let me introduce you to the Newsmaker. She makes news using new tools at her disposal. She is a journalist, but right now, she's also being asked to be a technologist. She represents what the media industry is becoming: an arena for story-enabling, not just storytelling. She is every journalist and every newsroom who wants not only to survive but to thrive in this current era of digital change.

The Newsmaker has worked at a well-established news company for several years, based in a city I'll call Fairview, reporting on different issues and producing important stories. Recently, an editor called her into his office and told her he would like to find a way to leverage artificial intelligence technology to create efficiencies in the newsroom.

The Newsmaker has no clue what this is.

To her, artificial intelligence is something that happens at high-tech start-ups, but now she is being tasked with implementing AI into her own reporting. Though this may seem a complex topic, there's no reason for alarm just yet. A few hours of online research give the Newsmaker an initial grasp of what AI is—smart machines enabled by computer formulas know as algorithms able to reason at the level of a human being.

These are some examples of the different ways news organizations are deploying AI in the service of journalism:

- *Forbes* developed an AI-powered content management system to automatically suggest headlines or images that should accompany a story.[1]

- The *Washington Post* uses a reporting bot that spots newsworthy data patterns, such as in financial trends or election results, leading journalists to scoops.

- The Associated Press uses smart technology to turn data into preview stories for every NBA game, without human involvement, freeing up sports reporters' time so they can focus on pieces that are unique, such as investigations.[2]

- The *Wall Street Journal*'s paywall is powered by an algorithm that predicts when a new reader is likely to subscribe.[3] This has enabled the business publication to grow both its revenues and audience.

- And in an even more futuristic use case: China's Xinhua News Agency created the world's first AI news anchor, a digital replica that resembles a human journalist.[4]

To some extent these systems are "editorial algorithms," which produce news outputs, thus requiring a level of oversight by humans.

After this initial research, the Newsmaker still has all sorts of unanswered questions. For example, if software is used to generate stories, who gets the byline? Where does the data come from? How does this process work? What quality control practices need to be put in place when using AI in the newsroom? Will she lose her job to a machine?

These are all questions the Newsmaker needs to answer before implementing anything. The Newsmaker isn't alone in asking them. Technological evolution moves faster than journalism can. And this is not a reason to blame journalism, because ultimately, the industry cannot match the speed of technological advances while maintaining sound editorial standards. There is an inevitable and *necessary* time lag.

FIGURE 0.1: Journalistic standards require time to adapt to technological innovation.

INTRODUCTION

Today's Newsmaker faces a journalism landscape similar to that of the late 1990s, when there were major shifts in the news industry, driven by the internet boom, that forced news organizations to navigate an entirely different consumption paradigm. Many newspapers started their digital journeys by scanning their print papers and making them available online through PDF documents. As technology costs dropped and digital skills improved, news companies developed more sophisticated models of producing and distributing content online, giving birth to today's dynamic digital landscape. According to the U.S. Bureau of Labor Statistics, 2016 marked the first time there were more jobs in internet publishing than in newspapers. The growth of digital media represented an industry shift unlike any we had seen before.[5]

AI promises to transform the entire journalistic workflow even more exponentially. The fast pace of technological development means that newsrooms will require near-constant learning and training to stay up to date.

The word "disruption" gets applied to a lot of glittery new tech these days, but the verb form refers to a specific point of market adoption. When something is "disrupted," it means the traditional method or approach has become less than optimal for mass consumption. The key term in this definition is "mass." Nothing is disruptive by virtue of being innovative or merely new. In fact, the simplest of solutions can disrupt industries if they become adopted by the bulk of users or consumers over a short period of time.

The internet disrupted the media industry only when the least likely users finally adopted it. With a critical mass of online consumers, news organizations were forced to introduce new digital production practices and update their business models.

While some organizations succeeded in their digital transformation efforts and the reskilling of their staff, others continued to experience eroding revenues—due to an inability to quickly adjust to audience needs as well as to increased competition.

Artificial intelligence is no different; at this point, AI is just starting to proliferate, and the Newsmaker wants to stay ahead of the curve. In this context, she has questions about the sustainability of newsrooms. How can she make news-gathering more efficient? And how can she scale high-impact journalism?

The answers to these questions may lie in the ability of the news industry to adopt and adapt to new technology. Disruption is often driven by large tech companies that are able to invest heavily in new infrastructure. According to a 2016 study published by O'Reilly Media, 33 percent of software and technology firms were investing in AI that year while only 1.33 percent of online media—including newspapers and other publishers—were doing so.[6] A 2017 report from the International Center for Journalists found that only 5 percent of newsroom staff have technology-related degrees, while only 2 percent of newsrooms employ technologists and only 1 percent employ analytics editors.[7]

Rather than trying to compete with the tech giants, to develop wholly new technology, the Newsmaker needs to learn how to quickly apply AI-powered tools to create sustainable journalism.

So here's what to expect.

The rise of artificial intelligence technology is quickly affecting newsgathering, production, and distribution.

It calls for new skills, tools, and workflows. But this does not mean that newsrooms will empty and become offices for smart machines. The future will look a lot more like a new form of collaboration: between humans and machines.

- **NEWSGATHERING:** artificial intelligence allows sourcing of information and story ideas through new types of collection processes, including machine learning that finds outliers within data, that automatically detects trends within social media user–generated content, and that extracts information from documents.

- **PRODUCTION:** reporters can now explore opportunities to automatically produce content, employ algorithms to switch between media formats (e.g., turning data into text and text into video), and repurpose content customized to various audiences.

- **DISTRIBUTION:** AI paves the way for journalists to meet news consumers in emerging platforms by understanding their behaviors and optimizing publishing and monetization strategies in real time.

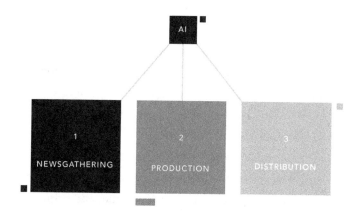

FIGURE 0.2: Artificial intelligence impacts all value points of journalism.

A FAST-CHANGING CONSUMPTION LANDSCAPE

In a recent brainstorming session with a colleague in the newsroom, the Newsmaker discussed how consumers and their habits are changing. She brings up the *Digital News Report 2018*, from the Reuters Institute for the Study of Journalism, which found that the portion of people who considered social media a source of news nearly doubled from 2013 to 2016, when it reached 46 percent.[8] The Newsmaker explains that the same study found that 39 percent of people now read online content as the first source of daily news, instead of a physical paper.

The world has entered a definable new era for production and consumption, a period some analysts have called "hyperinnovation" and "hyperadoption."[9]

The fact that consumers are adopting new things more

readily is affecting all kinds of consumption, including news.

The Newsmaker has witnessed this firsthand. Over the course of several years, her audience's preferences have completely transformed. Not only do they like different content—that's to be expected, since culture and society are dynamic—but they like different types of formats delivered in different ways across different platforms.

A survey from the American Press Institute found that while older people rely on television, radio, and print news, younger news consumers turn to online sources for news. For those in the eighteen to twenty-nine age range, their cell phones were as significant as news sources as their televisions.[10] Meanwhile, the *Digital News Report 2018* showed that younger demographics were more likely than older ones to find their news through social media and search engines than through direct access, with 53 percent of the eighteen to twenty-four age group using social media as a gateway to news, compared to only 33 percent of the fifty-five-plus group.[11]

These new consumption patterns are now in full force, creating a radically new context for news producers and consumers alike. The Newsmaker sees this as an opportunity. She wants to implement AI technology not because it's the inevitable "next big thing," but because she recognizes ways it can solve a major newsroom pain point: the need to cater to many audiences at the same time.

Artificial intelligence enables the Newsmaker to put out much more dynamic, personalized, customized reporting—looking into subtle data patterns, creating multimedia experiences, and mining for stories the naked eye can't see. For instance, the Xinhua New Agency's AI-powered platform "Media Brain" analyzes publicly and privately collected data from social media, search engines, news feeds, and more, allowing journalists to not only monitor potential news events but also optimize content production and distribution.[12]

As AI across the industry drives companies to reinvent themselves at breakneck speeds and the risks associated with trying something new or different are drastically reduced, customers are getting used to an accelerated cycle of change. In fact, risk becomes the status quo. Supported by new technologies, content producers can pass on fewer costs to their customers and thereby lower the customer's financial or emotional risks of adoption.

The Newsmaker realizes just how quickly the news industry is being affected by this shift. For example, online, her newspaper's brand is now one among many; her ideas now have greater competition as a variety of legitimate news-sharing media are contending for users' attention. An informal blog is not an irrelevant competitor anymore. A well-established brand is no longer entitled to consumer loyalty. In the digital age, that loyalty must be earned continually.

The emergence of new smart technologies that make it easier for anyone to create and distribute content has substantially lowered the barriers to entry in the news business. Launching an online publication and growing an audience have become almost universally accessible because of the web.

Artificial intelligence is the latest driver in this shift, allowing content creators to automatically produce text or video from data, find hidden insights in documents, and optimize content distribution across platforms. Tokyo-based start-up JX Press leverages artificial intelligence to detect breaking news on social media, automatically creating "news bulletins for urgent information on accidents, natural disasters, and other incidents."[13] This novel process has enabled the company to break news, in advance of traditional newspapers and TV stations in Japan.[14]

As a result of these emerging processes, journalism organizations are not only competing with other publishers but also being challenged by new technologies that disrupt traditional workflows and commoditize news content.

With digital technology creating a constantly changing environment of innovation and adaptation, newsmakers like the one in this book need to reassess what they have to offer news consumers. They have to go beyond simply understanding how to leverage new technology in the workplace and actively embrace new ways of working to sustain their competitive advantage.

A PROACTIVE APPROACH TO RETHINKING NEWS

Designing the future of news requires careful optimism: an acute awareness of existing limitations in the industry alongside curiosity and enthusiasm about innovation.

The Newsmaker's colleagues are less optimistic than she is. They perceive a prohibitive lack of agility in the newsroom when it comes to technological innovations.

While the Newsmaker understands the cynicism that

pervades some journalism organizations, she also knows that her company doesn't need to replicate Silicon Valley to thrive in the current media environment. The start-up industrial complex often makes media executives think that emulating small, high-growth organizations is the only way for a company to remain viable, but that isn't true. It's equally important to look for ways an organization can become more nimble within an existing ecosystem. The goal: be more agile than the day before.

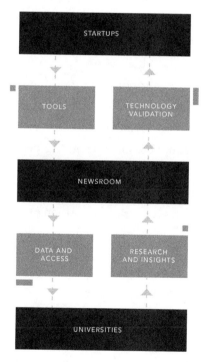

FIGURE 0.3: Newsrooms can collaborate with external partners, including startups and universities, to experiment with new technologies.

Well-established news organizations like the one the Newsmaker works for have a tendency to rely too much on their existing brands, histories, and reputations instead of proactively seeking new growth opportunities. One way newsmakers can reverse this institutional inertia is by meeting with researchers and start-up founders who might have fresh ideas for their organizations. Since new companies are often eager to have established newsrooms test their technology or implement their research, this can lead to mutually beneficial collaboration based on knowledge sharing rather than a significant monetary exchange.

Some of the ideas or products resulting from these collaborations might not prove useful, but journalists ultimately benefit from learning to look beyond the newsroom walls for solutions. And collaborative projects are not the only potential upside: sourcing outside perspectives can also create new jobs based in cooperation between tech companies, research centers, and newsrooms. For example, the Associated Press has created a position exclusively dedicated to newsroom partnerships, a role responsible for sourcing opportunities for collaborations with universities, start-ups, and other media organizations.[15]

A SHIFT IN HOW WE ACCESS NEWS AND INFORMATION

The Newsmaker and her colleagues operate in a journalism landscape where the relationship between news and its audiences has changed dramatically in recent decades.

Unlike radio and television, which were traditionally appointment-driven platforms, where users convened at a specific time and place, the internet enables on-demand experiences. And it's always in flux. Platforms like television, print, and radio, which allowed media companies to provide unique content to their audiences, are quickly evolving into something entirely different.

What does that mean for the Newsmaker's organization? And for its audience?

In an oversupplied news ecosystem, publishers sense an obligation not only to produce more content in order to meet the needs of multiple audiences but also to differentiate themselves through unique story angles and mediums for publication.

The Newsmaker must increasingly ask of herself and her colleagues what it means to tell stories compellingly. In a digital context, this is not only about a style of writing or narrative novelty but about how content is distributed and presented across new platforms.

This fiercely competitive environment also shapes how news consumers perceive the world around them. The democratization of online publishing and the growth of social distribution are enabling consumers to switch quickly between different news media sources and platforms. This is what's driving a heated contest between news publications striving to be the go-to source for certain topics or areas of coverage. To this end, some newsrooms forecast trends and bet on a few popular topics.[16]

But if there are a lot of participants in this news contest, and some stories everyone feels obligated to chase, the Newsmaker and her colleagues also have a higher chance of being a go-to source, by choosing stories that have not been covered extensively.

For the Newsmaker, this feels like a decision between popularity and journalistic necessity.

The dilemma is far too common in newsrooms. And it creates an incentive to publish stories on topics that are at one of two extremes: marginal or hyperpolarizing. Neither is productive for fostering a healthy public discourse. This conundrum is, in some cases, exacerbated by personalization algorithms that tailor content to the profile of each individual. When users are only shown stories on topics they already care about, and thus are not exposed to a diverse range of viewpoints, this can lead to a one-dimensional media diet and ultimately to a reinforcement of preconceived ideas.

In the age of smart machines, journalists have an important role in helping readers navigate a complex information ecosystem. Human news judgment can ensure that audiences are able to stay informed about topics that are of public interest.

For the Newsmaker it's crucial to build a sustainable model for journalism, a model that is able to keep up with technological change while staying true to editorial values and serving as a reference point for society.

FINDING THE RIGHT MODEL

Building a sustainable model for news is increasingly important as the market experiences a shift of advertising dollars from news companies to big tech platforms.

According to a 2018 *eMarketer* report, Facebook, Google, and Amazon are now reaping over 62 percent of U.S. digital advertising revenues, as they aggregate massive audiences without incurring significant costs of content development (when compared to their overall structure).[17] Meanwhile, technology companies like Apple are quickly becoming dominant players for paid premium content, with its Apple News+ service offering subscriptions to publications such as the *Wall Street Journal* and the *Los Angeles Times*.

The symbiosis between journalism and technology—two worlds with historically different cultures and business models—is creating both tension and opportunity. Analysis by researchers Kevin Drew and Ryan Thomas at the Missouri School of Journalism suggests that although the separation of newsroom and business departments has been at the core of journalistic integrity, financial challenges driven by the digital transformation have led to more collaboration across departments.[18]

News organizations are behaving like start-ups, and journalists are expanding their skills beyond just reporting. They are leveraging data, building products, learning about the business side, and exploring new platforms to distribute content and grow their audiences. It's no surprise that organizations promoting technical literacy in journalism, such as Journocoders or Hacks/Hackers, and data journalism conferences, such as those hosted by the National Institute for Computer-Assisted Reporting, are becoming so popular in the industry.

But news organizations still need audience reach, a large amount of news stories, and editorial differentiation. These traditional tenets of the news industry have remained relevant. Now, however, newsrooms also need increasingly efficient ways of producing content and new business models that generate revenue in a digital landscape.

As the following sections of this book argue, artificial intelligence is an important way news organizations can achieve these goals.

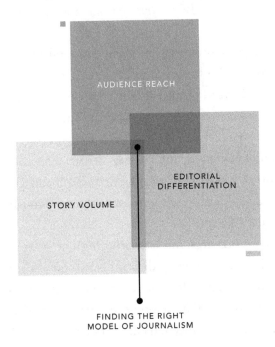

FINDING THE RIGHT
MODEL OF JOURNALISM

FIGURE 0.4: In an oversupplied and highly competitive media ecosystem, news organizations must find the balance between each reach, volume, and differentiation.

Now is the time for newsrooms to take advantage of technology like AI, which can help diversify content formats, create workflow efficiencies, and distribute news across platforms. Most importantly, now is the time to embrace a new approach to change: the iterative process.

1

THE PROBLEM

A JOURNALISTIC MODEL
IN TRANSITION

While not long ago the scenario that follows might have seemed like a fantasy, one could easily imagine it happening in a few years, thanks to advancements in AI.

It's the near future. When the Newsmaker wakes up, so do all the smart devices in her home. One device starts playing the Newsmaker's daily news digest, timed precisely for the moment she has left the bed and taken a few steps. It knows her brain isn't ready for full-length news stories right when she wakes up.

Meanwhile, her smart house begins preparing for the day. An algorithmic coffee maker brews a cup personalized to the Newsmaker's tastes. Her smartphone prepares a preview of the day's calendar, and before she has left the house she has already been updated on the relevant news affecting her beat.

Outside, the Newsmaker hops into her self-driving car. On the ride to work, a podcast playlist has been algorithmically customized based on her consumption patterns.

A few miles from work, the car's sensors detect a 10 percent reduction in air quality. This intrigues the Newsmaker. As she nears the newsroom, an algorithm that tracks social media notifies her that there's increased chatter online about air pollution and children suffering from asthma attacks in the area.

Once she's inside the office, she turns to her AI-powered software to access targeted data: a network of drones measure air quality and take aerial photos. She gets the following automated assessment:

> There has been a decrease in visibility—a potential
> indicator of high air pollution—within 5 miles
> of the textiles factories in the past 10 days.

Meanwhile, the Newsmaker commands an AI software to assess historical datasets looking for correlations, some of which the Newsmaker hasn't even asked for. An analysis of the National Institute of Environmental Health Sciences database highlights that pollution rates in the region are abnormally high when compared to historical trends.

At the same time, another AI is detecting clusters of

conversations on social media from parents concerned about the health of their children. The system quickly summarizes trends in the discussion.

The Newsmaker decides to explore these findings using qualitative interviews with local sources. Some of her sources are people she has spoken to before, while others the AI suggested and located, including the manager of a local textile factory.

Later, an AI automatically transcribes the audio for all her interviews, saving the Newsmaker hours of manual work. She also wants to be sure she understood her sources correctly, so she deploys her AI to evaluate the consistency of all statements. Everything matches up.

After gathering qualitative and quantitative data, the Newsmaker is almost ready to publish a story. She directs another AI to generate a first draft that aggregates the data and summarizes previous news reports on air pollution in the area. The program teases out the story for the Newsmaker; she reviews it and makes a few edits. After the article is reviewed by an automation editor who understands the nature of how this story has been created, the piece is published across various platforms. Headline: "Fairview Parents Concerned about Health Damage from Air Pollution."

This initial story gets substantial traction and many of her readers demand more information about the situation. Analyzing the article's comments section, the relevant AI identifies a number of concerned citizens discussing whether there was negligence from the local factory owners. That's a good angle for a story, she thinks.

The new model of journalism is most effective when

it integrates real-time feedback from audiences. But this means reporters must adapt their workflow to a more engaged and dynamic form of storytelling. In this scenario, AI was used to find relevant insights and most importantly to test whether the topic is of interest to readers before investing too many resources into a full journalistic investigation. This is iterative journalism.

Machines will not replace the most important roles of the journalist. Instead, they will fuel reporters, providing more opportunities to go deeper into stories and actively connect with readers. While the transition won't be easy, the personal contributions of the journalist will remain central to the process.

Welcome to the new world of the Newsmaker.[1] This is a world of human-machine collaboration, where data is leveraged as raw material, as distinct from content. Where it can be collected from sensors, mined from news archives, and analyzed by algorithms to extract insights.

It's a world that open-sources information gathering and treats the news consumer's feedback as an integral part of the process. A world in which newsmakers have the freedom to be more creative, by adapting to new kinds of information dissemination. Whether they will take advantage of their newfound freedom is another question.

1.1. THE OLD JOURNALISM MODEL

Throughout its history, journalism has operated linearly—reporters conceived a story idea through laborious research and data analysis, cultivated and interviewed sources, packaged all of this information into a draft, then worked with editors to finalize their one-off articles (with limited distribution across platforms). Eventually, much later, the story is published. Only after publication did readers come into contact with that piece of journalism.

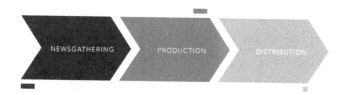

FIGURE 1.1: The traditional journalism model is linear, rigid, and structured.

For the Newsmaker, the procedural inefficiency of this process was only the beginning of the problem.

Historically, the Newsmaker was unable to get audience feedback for stories that were still being written and refined. She was only scratching the surface of the data she had available; looking for complex correlations within it wasn't feasible for a person with tight deadlines.

In the context of modern media consumption, the limitations of this traditional model have become painfully obvious. Its rigidity prevents journalists from identifying relevant new perspectives in a story because there's little opportunity to consider ideas before the piece is published.

We can segment the Newsmaker's core activities in this traditional model into three processes: gathering information, packaging that information into a story, and, finally, distributing the story through her newspaper, in print or online. Each of these processes could benefit from AI.

NEWSGATHERING WAS SLOW AND LIMITED BY MANUAL PROCESSES

In the traditional model of researching and writing a story, the Newsmaker used her own archives, publicly available data, and reliable sources she has called on over the years— the city clerk, key community leaders, the president of the county's industrial association, and so on.

The Newsmaker had a list of sources and stuck to them. Actually, she was stuck *with* them. They were her network, and although it was extensive, in many cases, it never felt big or diverse enough.

She conducted interviews in person, by phone, or by email, took notes on a laptop, manually transcribed audio recordings, and drafted stories using a word processor. For one story previously described, she sifted through thousands of data points and reports about factory pollution from the state's environmental agency. This alone took her hours. Sometimes she found herself thinking that she didn't graduate with a journalism degree just to transcribe phone calls.

The entire process of news collection was slow, manual, and heavily reliant on institutional knowledge developed by the editorial staff. Institutional knowledge is not a bad thing, as long as it doesn't become institutionalized past the point of no return. In this case, technology, external data, and audience feedback that could have made reporting more efficient were ignored simply because the Newsmaker was pressed for time, due to the structural inefficiencies of her newsroom.

Before integrating AI and other new technologies into her own work, the Newsmaker assesses the risks of relying strictly on traditional methods for data collection. She knows that if she had more data, her stories would have included additional context, but she also knows that her time is limited. Reading user comments on the website (some of which are . . . not so nice), she realizes that her reporting could have explored other angles that would be relevant to her audiences.

How distinct would her stories have been if real-time audience feedback and sophisticated AI-powered software were available just a few years ago?

A story she wrote on college campus safety—which took two months of research and writing—would have benefited from real-time updates on the increased number of complaints from universities around the state. If she had developed that story using emerging tools that scrape publicly accessible databases and documents, she could have incorporated constant input on how these safety incidents continued to affect the schools.

This data might have come from social listening tools, algorithms that track conversation shifts on Twitter, Facebook, and online forums, or public reports sent out by universities themselves.

At the same time, this sensitive data would not have gone directly to publication before the Newsmaker reviewed it. This is why it's not AI alone that enables rich reporting, but the combination of journalistic intuition and machine intelligence.

FIGURE 1.2: Human machine collaboration; combining people's intuition with computer's intelligence

The future of newsrooms depends on investments in both human and technological capital. A survey conducted in 2018 by the Reuters Institute for the Study of Journalism showed that 78 percent of respondents believe that investment in AI is needed, while 85 percent believed that human journalists will help newsrooms navigate future challenges.[2]

In the new model of human-machine collaboration, storytelling becomes dynamic. In the Newsmaker's campus safety story, as the number of reported incidents rose, the content could have been automatically refreshed to convey the more dire situation. With AI, the story would have been written once but contextualized with new data on an ongoing basis—under the supervision of an editor.

Under the traditional model, the Newsmaker and her colleagues all tended to approach a story in a similar way. They scoured the data to find anomalies and then cross-referenced those anomalies with interviews. What they were missing is that anomalies in data or conflicting source perspectives are not always meaningful. Maybe, more importantly, the contrapositive is also true: just because a data point is not an anomaly doesn't make it insignificant. This is where machines are now helping the Newsmaker.

In a 2017 investigation into spy planes, BuzzFeed News trained a machine-learning model to look for aircrafts with flight patterns similar to those operated by the Department of Homeland Security and the FBI.[3] The system, which was trained on data from twenty thousand planes, looked for attributes such as flight speed, altitude, and duration. Although the algorithm allowed the reporter to accurately identify new surveillance airplanes operated by law enforcement agencies, it also produced some inaccurate results. In some instances, the AI thought skydiving operations were spy planes, because of similarities in their flight patterns— navigating in a small area for a given period of time. The machine made a mistake that was caught by thorough human oversight.

As described above, leveraging new methods of data analysis, story sourcing, and machine-driven audience analytics can lead news organizations to new coverage topics, add a greater level of context to their reporting, and open a channel of transparency and conversation with their audience.

For example, the *Financial Times* used AI to develop "She Said He Said," a bot that automatically tracks whether a source quoted in a written story is male or female.[4] The system works by using text analysis algorithms that track pronouns and first names to determine the gender of people mentioned in any given article. As reporters write their piece, the bot will alert them of any imbalance in gender ratios. A previous project, JanetBot, leveraged computer vision to identify men and women in the images on the *Financial Times* home page.[5] According to FT these efforts are based on "research showing a positive correlation between stories including quotes of women and higher rates of engagement with female readers."

At the same time, choosing not to leverage external data or audience feedback is detrimental to news organizations, as it runs the risk of creating an echo chamber that precludes opportunities to uncover new story subjects and angles or diversify the audience.

THE TRADITIONAL PROCESS IS A ONE-SIZE-FITS-ALL SOLUTION

For the story on college campus safety, the Newsmaker only had time to develop one angle, for one audience—the same ambiguously defined audience she has always written for. Like many journalists have done for years, the Newsmaker was trained to write for an imagined audience, one based on limited knowledge of who her readers actually were.

An article entitled "Fairview University On-Campus Safety Incidents Force Chancellor to Resign," for example, would appear in the same form to a twenty-year-old woman who attends Fairview University as it does to the middle-aged father of a high school senior in the neighboring town of Franklin whose child is applying to college. The content was one-size-fits-all. And why wouldn't it be? The Newsmaker wrote stories in the hopes of reaching as many people as possible. She couldn't write five different stories, tailored to five different readers or platforms—she didn't have the time or the resources.

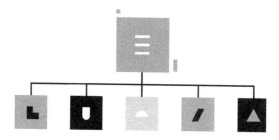

FIGURE 1.3: The traditional novel relies on a "one-size-fits-all" approach to journalism where different readers are exposed to the same piece of content.

In this traditional model, one-size-fits-all makes sense. A good portion of what journalists produce is a result of time-consuming processes, from writing to video to photography, all generated without the help of smart technology. In this model, human input is the dominant driver of the process.

But this approach is misaligned with the current media landscape. Oversupplied with content and undersupplied with technology, publishers must learn to respect the value of differentiation. The old model of media, which was once adequate, is becoming less so because people's expectations and options for information sources are now widened. Human journalists alone cannot support the growing demand for personalization.

After being reviewed by an editor, the Newsmaker's campus safety story was published. In the old model, circulation was limited to distribution channels where the newsroom had full oversight: the weekly print paper, the website, a mobile app, and, in some cases, links on social media in hopes of driving traffic back to the home page.

This scenario illustrates just how linear the traditional model of journalism is—gathering information, creating a story for a specific use, and distributing it as a final product. But as new technologies enter the bloodstream of society, they can accelerate how newsrooms operate, setting the stage for a new model of journalism.

1.2. THE NEW JOURNALISM MODEL

Back in the present (and the future), the Newsmaker finally has the tools she needs to reimagine what storytelling can look like.

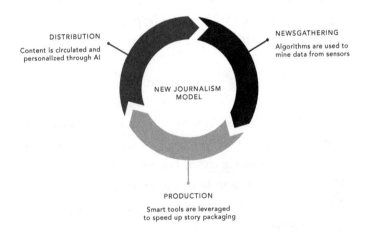

DISTRIBUTION
Content is circulated and
personalized through AI

NEWSGATHERING
Algorithms are used to
mine data from sensors

NEW JOURNALISM
MODEL

PRODUCTION
Smart tools are leveraged
to speed up story packaging

FIGURE 1.4: The modern journalism workflow is dynamic, with each step of the process being augmented by AI.

With AI-powered tools readily available, the new paradigm of journalism breaks away from the linear succession of "gather, package, and distribute" for each story. It atomizes each step and augments it with new technology.

NEWSGATHERING TAKES SHAPE
OUTSIDE THE NEWSROOM WALLS

At a recent industry conference focused on journalism innovation, the Newsmaker learned about a number of new approaches that allow journalists to source and verify content created by anyone, regardless of topic, format, or location.

She became particularly fascinated with how user-generated content, drone footage, and data from sensors can provide intelligence from the field, oftentimes from areas reporters can't access. Even without any background in artificial intelligence, the Newsmaker was growing more confident that she could integrate these new content sources into her own work. To her, the sources were complementary, not in competition.

Taking the long view, the Newsmaker recalled how the telephone had become an important newsgathering tool by the mid-1930s.[6] It allowed reporters to contact sources more quickly and increased their reach far beyond the previous range. The same argument could be made for artificial intelligence today: it's just another tool in the editorial Swiss Army knife.

For example, using the AI-powered platform News Tracer, Reuters has been able to sift through emerging topics on social media to determine if they are newsworthy and truthful, which helps reporters monitor events and find relevant stories more quickly. The tool has been particularly relevant for breaking news situations. In 2015, it revealed social media activity documenting a shooting in San Bernardino, California, before any other news organization. The next year, News Tracer warned its journalists of an earthquake in Ecuador eighteen minutes before other publishers broke the story.[7]

EYEWITNESSES ARE EVERYWHERE

The rise of social media platforms has given birth to an ecosystem where text posts, photos, and video provide an eyewitness perspective on major breaking news events big and small—from terrorist attacks to parades and the local high school football team victory. This happens at an unprecedented scale and with unprecedented speed.

By mining feeds from social media and other public sources, AI also enables the Newsmaker to uncover new perspectives for existing stories. It allows journalists to use the entire digital sphere as one giant source of structured information.

For example, Spanish newspaper *El País* leveraged data mining tool Graphext to map relationships between politicians and the media, by analyzing hundreds of social media accounts.[8]

Like Reuters, public broadcaster Radio France collaborated with a technology company, Dataminr, to leverage an AI-powered tool to detect outliers in social media conversations. This gave the French news organization a head start covering the 2016 bombing of the Brussels airport and the terrorist attack in Nice, because social media functioned like an early warning system for uncovering emerging narrative threads.[9] This type of early detection gave its journalists more time to plan and respond to breaking news stories.

The Newsmaker can now use updates published by citizens on social media to measure public discourse, including people's sentiments about the problems at the Fairview factories described above. Reviewing social media, public records, news archives and forums, and other sources faster than the Newsmaker can blink, AI brings a new perspective to journalism.

A recent alert sent to the Newsmaker from one of these systems read:

> Mothers in East Fairview are referencing opioid death with abnormal frequency—up 250% since last week.

This type of AI tool works by clustering together people who share similar demographic or psychographic profiles and then running semantic analysis (the meaning behind language) on the updates they post online. This approach is a process by which machines can group similar content together by analyzing patterns in their words.

This new approach can provide publishers with news emerging directly from citizens' concerns via social media feeds and help journalists respond to the issues and events that are affecting their audiences' lives at any given moment.

However, as citizens' concerns over data privacy deepen we will experience the growth of more private, closed social networks like WhatsApp, Signal, and WeChat, which will impact this type of monitoring of social media by journalists. In fact, The *Digital News Report 2018* found that private messaging was growing as a news source, with the portion of people using WhatsApp for news doubling in the past four years, to 16 percent.[10] A Pew Research Center study found that 44 percent of young people aged eighteen to twenty-nine have deleted the Facebook app from their phone and 64 percent have adjusted their privacy settings in the last year.[11] These trends suggest that crowdsourced reporting will have to continually adapt, in particular to a landscape where discussions of the news take place through private mediums.

One new AI-powered tool used by the Newsmaker can monitor all media outlets (whether via social media, RSS feeds, web scraping, or some other source) to determine who's covering what topics, what's being investigated, when it happened, and where it takes place:

> UK prime minister mentions by conservative news outlets are up 5% today, compared to its weekly average. The news articles discuss concepts related to budget and healthcare reform.

To put it simply, this feed provides the Newsmaker and her colleagues with news about the news. Inside the AI, various computer programs track major media outlets while other programs analyze their content. The AI, which has been trained on many news articles, is able to read and identify topics, sentiment, and other useful features. All this, which would take the Newsmakers hours to read through, the AI can sort and surface in an efficient manner.

With it, the Newsmaker and her colleagues know who

is covering what and, most importantly, how, which in turn allows them to better differentiate their own reporting to reach the widest possible audience with the strongest, most distinctive angle.

The technologies described above are not science fiction. The *Wall Street Journal* mines news archives from Factiva, a database with over thirty-three thousand sources, to monitor the ever-changing landscape of regulation and financial crime. A tool called Media Cloud, developed by researchers at MIT's Center for Civic Media and used by emerging news organizations like Vocativ and *FiveThirtyEight*, found that during the 2013–2016 Ebola outbreak, there was more public engagement with stories about infections in the United States than with those about infections in West Africa, where the disease was most deadly, which highlighted the challenges facing global health organizations attempting to direct the narrative about the Ebola outbreak.[12]

There have never been enough reporters in the newsroom, not to mention enough time in the day, to research every possible news story or possible angle. In the traditional model, the Newsmaker had a tendency to get stuck in the same news cycle (bad weather, political scandal, company going out of business, local hero, and so on), but machine learning tools can help create a more diversified news agenda and sourcing practices by holding a mirror up to the publication's own coverage. Any data point (from social media to public records and official documents, from press releases to news archives) can be used to further the journalistic mission.

In collaboration with the Laboratory for Social Machines at the MIT Media Lab, Vice News developed a story demonstrating the political divide on Twitter leading up to the 2016 U.S. presidential election.[13] The MIT researchers built a series of classifiers (smart filters) to categorize Twitter users by their political ideology and location, using a type of artificial intelligence called *supervised learning*. Through this approach, it was possible to understand the structure and dynamics of users' relationships across the political divide. Vice News was able to surface that Donald Trump supporters formed "a particular insular group when talking about politics," while Hillary Clinton proponents were far less cohesive as a group. While the data did not predict the outcome of the election, it provided journalists an unprecedented analytical insight into how information bubbles might have contributed to the polarization of public discourse during a crucial period in our recent history.

The complexity of these data results shows that no matter how sophisticated such systems become, humans will still have a central role in defining best practices for the machines and interpreting results. It's the Newsmaker's responsibility to understand how the algorithms make causal links between data sets, to recognize when a source may prove valuable, and to know when to push forward with or step back from a story.

EMERGING FORMS OF NEWSGATHERING

The Newsmaker doesn't only draw on existing human sources. She is also testing how to collect additional information through new techniques. Smart devices, like the sensors in her car or data beacons used to track movement, can also be

QUESTIONS TO ASK
WHEN APPLYING AI IN
THE NEWSROOM

- **CHALLENGE:** What challenges are you trying to solve?

- **PROCESS:** How can you translate this challenge into smaller steps?

- **DATA:** Do you have the right data to solve the challenge?

- **RESEARCH:** Where is the data coming from and how is it going to be vetted?

- **PITFALLS:** What errors can be expected from the algorithm and how can you add editorial oversight?

used to provide more context to a story.

Smart sensors can offer her data on traffic, weather, population density, or power consumption. With other, similar smart devices, the Newsmaker can monitor vibration and noise from entertainment and political events to identify the most popular songs at a concert, the biggest plays of a game, or the quotes that resonate most with people attending campaign rallies. Or she could monitor vibrations of construction sites to measure the impact on nearby residents and businesses, or track foot traffic at new public transportation stops, to gauge their usage.

The *South Florida Sun Sentinel* collected data through GPS sensors to investigate speeding police officers, leading to a series awarded a Pulitzer Prize for Public Service in 2013.[14] The public radio program *Radiolab* leveraged temperature sensors to predict the arrival of cicadas as well as to evaluate the impact of heat stress in the neighborhood of Harlem in New York City.[15]

Some news organizations are even experimenting with AI-powered sensors. In partnership with NYU's Studio 20 journalism program, researcher Stephanie Ho developed a prototype with the Associated Press of a sensor-powered camera for reporters and photographers working at large-scale public events.[16] The sensor would monitor the space for triggers, like noise, and when the triggers reached a certain threshold the sensor would take a photograph and email it to the reporter.

These developments are exciting to journalists like the Newsmaker. But many newsrooms find them threatening, seeing in them the demise of the profession. A more nuanced perspective is that this technological evolution does not replace the traditional approach of researching stories. It actually increases newsrooms' access to data and insights.

Meanwhile, with the help of universities or through collaborations with technology companies, experimenting with AI is becoming more accessible. These partnerships can be established by hosting university research fellows in the newsroom and by establishing capstone courses with journalism schools. Another effective approach for underfinanced news organizations looking to innovate in a cost-effective manner is to seek grants from foundations. For instance, the *Seattle Times* received financing from the Knight Foundation's AI and the News: Open Challenge to develop a reporting project evaluating the implications of machine learning on work and labor.[17]

Partnering with a university researcher, the Newsmaker employs an AI system to investigate whether a $40 million investment in the train station in Fairview was a good use of public funds. The city's transportation commissioner recently deemed the project a resounding "success," claiming that the station's average daily use rate is 3,000 people. By installing sophisticated AI-powered sensors that monitor the number of people who enter and leave the station, and employing an AI-enabled computer to detect and analyze images for certain objects, such as people, the Newsmaker is able to determine that the real usage rate is, in fact, closer to 1,500—half the figure the public official announced.

That data point nudges the Newsmaker to investigate further, by requesting public records on the volume of ticket sales and interviewing workers at the station. The resulting journalistic work is published with the headline, "Transportation Commissioner Inflates Passenger Estimate."

In this instance, using AI-powered technology helped the Newsmaker keep a public official accountable.

The *New York Times* also deployed this kind of technology, to illustrate the power and perils of image recognition.[18] Using public video footage of Bryant Park in New York City and analyzing it through Amazon's facial recognition software (which is commercially available), journalists were able to identify thousands of faces of people who were caught on camera walking by the park. The result is an interactive article discussing the broader implications of this type of technology and its potential uses by governments. Most surprisingly, the story features interviews with some of those individuals who were initially tracked by the *New York Times*'s AI system.

Similar technologies applied by newsmakers are also helping their newsrooms become more efficient. Instead of spending valuable work hours transcribing interviews and manually inputting datasets, a reporter's daily duties could be focused on making important calls and pursuing leads derived from AI insights. The reporter should be the reporter, not the assistant *and* the reporter.

Using AI, the Newsmaker also has the tools and computing power she needs to recognize causal links or correlations within data that she would not have noticed on her own. But even though AI flags these points of connection, it is still up to her to verify and unpack relationships within

SANITY CHECKS JOURNALISTS CAN FOLLOW TO EVALUATE AI-DRIVEN RESULTS

- **CONSISTENCY:** Ensure that the output is plausible and aligns with an initial understanding of the data. This means confirming that the level of magnitude of a certain result is appropriate (e.g., thousands of people vs. hundreds of people).

- **REPLICABILITY:** Make sure it is possible to reproduce the output if the results are probed by editors. Journalists should keep records of the data used, methodology, and final output.

- **VERIFY:** Have a colleague check and cross-reference final calculations. It is important to document the entire process, so that it can easily be explained to other journalists how a certain algorithmic result in a story was obtained.

the data.

Perhaps the AI detected only 1,500 people entering and leaving the train station at Fairview, but its motion sensors and image recognition software did not identify children in strollers. This is where human auditing is not only crucial for AI-driven systems—it's irreplaceable.

As AI technologies become prevalent, explainability becomes a high-demand feature when the public seeks to understand the technologies that govern their lives. Because algorithms are often written as black boxes, where only inputs and outputs are seen by their users, journalists must fill a role in explaining and examining these technologies. Therefore, even when AI is applied in an investigation, a human reporter is still crucial to the journalistic process.

DISTRIBUTING THE NEWS: NEWSROOMS ARE NOT BOUND BY A SINGLE OUTPUT TO TELL THE STORY

The Newsmaker notices that consumers are coming to the news from a variety of perspectives and platforms, with 68 percent of U.S. adults getting news from social media sites, according to a 2018 Pew Research Center study.[19] Her newly AI-powered newsroom can now provide multiple story angles that suit those distinct consumers.

Even more importantly, journalists can work with AI to reimagine news as dynamic, rather than static. Historically, the news relationship has been one-way, built around the terms and timelines of the publisher, and between the news organization and a single perceived audience.

Modern media consumers are looking for immediate value in terms of information and analysis; if they don't find it in one place, rather than invest in further interaction with the content, they will head elsewhere to learn about their world. Given that virtually all media providers are on the internet, this means that there's one unified "attention arena," with everyone is competing in the same environment. This wasn't the case two decades ago, when each medium had a distinct distribution channel: people watched programs on TV, listened to broadcasts on the radio, and read the news in the paper. Traditional news organizations are fighting for audiences and users' attention with all other sources of information, not just other journalistic organizations. And that means that news publishers need not only to differentiate themselves from one another but also to differentiate themselves *as an industry*, to make their content competitive with other media on the internet, including games, books, and movies.

The Newsmaker has been exploring new topics to cover and unique programming that can attract new audiences across different segments. She recently used a video automation tool to generate content in niche topics such as climate change, marijuana legalization, space exploration, and other topics her younger readers are particularly interested in.

Looking beyond AI, one strategy for setting publishers apart is to expand into emerging platforms that are not currently primary sources for news. For example, the *Washington Post* launched its "Playing Games with Politicians" series on Twitch (a popular platform used to stream video games), allowing users to follow along as politicians are interviewed while playing a video game.[20] Meanwhile, video game journalism is an emerging field where reporters work with video game designers to make the narratives and experiences the reporters cover into interactive applications. American Public Media's *Budget Hero* game, which allows users to attempt to balance the federal budget, is one example of innovative reporting using an emerging media form that combines information with entertainment.[21]

New formats in digital storytelling, many powered by AI, have grown exponentially as competition for audiences intensifies. The dominance of social media and mobile platforms, alongside algorithms that can create new versions of a story, has prompted a fundamental shift in storytelling structure.[22] Emerging and newly popularized entry points for news include imagery, timelines, social media cards, short video, virtual and augmented reality, newsletters, bots, data visualizations, listicles, long-form interactive stories, voice-enabled news, explorable explainers, alerts and notifications, and more. These new approaches do not replace traditional journalistic storytelling. In fact, they enable journalists to provide their audiences with more value and more access points to interact with information.

In 2016, news organizations including the Associated Press and Reuters leveraged AI-powered platform Graphiq to automatically generate data visualizations and insert them directly into articles to provide readers with additional context. This AI works by understanding the nature of the concepts in a story and pairing them with a relevant data visual. In some instances, publishers using this system registered a 40 percent increase in reader time on-site.[23] The resources and training to help manage emerging production processes and unlock all the advantage from using these AI tools.

FIGURE 1.5: Newsrooms must be able to produce multiple formats and distribute content across different platforms. Artificial intelligence enables journalists to do this at scale.

growth in new forms of storytelling may also require more

Given the industry-wide resource problems, how do journalists cultivate dynamic storytelling in light of time and economic constraints? The Newsmaker has discovered that one solution is the automatic creation of different versions of the same story.

By leveraging summarization technology, the Newsmaker can automatically turn a long article into a mobile-friendly post. This process relies on a type of AI called *natural language*, a class of algorithms that helps computers interpret and manipulate human language. In the case of AI-driven summaries, it works by ranking the relevance of phrases and automatically selecting the passages that convey the most critical information from the original news article.

The newsmaker can also effectively use AI to turn sports data into hundreds of text stories at scale, and even from different perspectives—say, from both the winning and the losing teams. This applies not only to the headline, but also to the story itself. In this case, the algorithms are helping the Newsmaker produce different versions of the same stories, something that, if done manually, would have been incredibly time-consuming.

Barcelona FC Knocked Out Again by Real Madrid

vs.

Real Madrid Continues Winning Streak Against Barcelona FC

The AI-powered news agency Narrativa, for example, is able to create 18,000 distinct soccer news articles for different leagues and teams, every week, in English, Spanish, and Arabic. These stories are then published by news portals such as MSN.com and *El Confidencial.*

Exploring this type of capability even leads the News-maker to create different story versions based on world region:

> In London today, the prime minister announced . . .
>
> In England's capital, London, the prime . . .
>
> In a briefing in front of Downing Street . . .

(**NOTE:** We will explain in detail how all of these technologies work in chapter 2.)

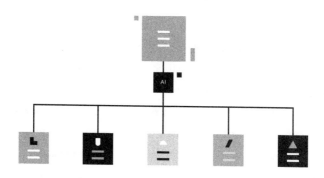

FIGURE 1.6: Artificial intelligence enables to personalize and localize content to individual news consumers.

While localization and personalization drive higher consumption, they can also create distortions of the public sphere if implemented without editorial guidelines and well-defined journalistic standards. For example, which of the following headlines do you perceive as being more critical? Which do you think a supporter of the opposing party is more likely to click?

> **HEADLINE 1:** *The Progressive Party* **Pushes** *a Bill Demanding Increased Financial Regulation*
>
> **HEADLINE 2:** *The Progressive Party* **Proposes** *a Bill Urging Further Financial Regulation*

Generating paraphrased text is still an emerging field in natural language processing. Basic techniques include using grammatical rules and thesaurus entries to replace words in a sentence. More complex methods use AI models that are trained to translate longer passages to shorter passages by learning patterns in word sequences for full and paraphrased texts. A similar approach can be used to tailor content according to its readers, varying personality, tone, location, time of day, and more.

One pitfall to note is that news consumers tend to seek content that confirms their preexisting beliefs—a phenomenon known as confirmation bias—which can lead them to share only their particular viewpoint on social media and contribute to a more polarized online discourse.[24] Newsrooms personalizing content from different perspectives should be cautious not to use these tools to feed more divisive consumption.

As long as journalists heed these precautions, newsrooms can leverage AI to advance their journalistic mission by extracting data from archives, mining it for insights, and even automatically personalizing it before distribution. Algorithms developed with artificial intelligence can convert data into stories and customize them to serve specific audience needs based on real-time feedback. Smart machines can make the process faster and more efficient. We live in a data-driven world. We always have. The only difference now is that we have the tools to measure, interpret, and process the data, and the time to develop deeper perspectives.

Automation allows news organizations to distribute higher volumes of content at lower costs, and also to produce entirely new content that would have otherwise been too expensive to create.

Needless to say, the promise of higher-quality outcomes without cost-cutting tactics is not new, nor is it necessarily unique to AI. During the industrial revolution, business magnates promised that machines would not replace human jobs, only alter them, while increasing the average quality of life exponentially. Machines would be doing the low-level jobs, leaving more complex and interesting work to the humans. But some companies used the efficiency of the new machines to reduce operational costs rather than reinvest in higher-level work. This is also a legitimate concern with regard to AI.

Encouragingly, research suggests that jobs that involve creativity, ideation, and empathy are those least likely to be automated. In a 2013 study, researchers at Oxford University found that the likelihood of computers taking over journalists' and newspaper editors' jobs was 8 percent, while for reporters and correspondents it was 11 percent.[25] Meanwhile, the likelihood that a bank clerk's position will be automated is 96.8 percent; for a sports coach, 38.3 percent.

A more proactive and strategic approach to this issue is exemplified by organizations such as the Associated Press, which since 2014 has used the savings it gained from automated financial stories (an estimated 20 percent of journalists' time saved[26]) to train reporters in immersive media and digital storytelling. Not only was there no job loss; there were new jobs created, such as that of automation editor.

EXPLORING NEW MODELS AND POINTS OF DISTRIBUTION

Since the advent of the internet, publishers have been trying to leverage distribution channels—such as social media networks—to drive traffic to their websites. Now content can be hosted, distributed, and monetized on these third-party platforms through services including Facebook's Instant Articles and Google's subscription tool for publishers. For example, an analysis conducted in 2016 by AI platform Naytev showed that BuzzFeed used forty-five different distribution channels, including messaging apps and image- and video-sharing platforms.[27] A staggering 80 percent of the publisher's reach existed beyond their website.

The Newsmaker has seen the emergence of a new wave of media companies such as NowThis that emphasize syndicating their content through third-party platforms. Is this the right approach? What about maintaining control of content and its standards?

When content is distributed beyond the publisher's

properties there is a real risk that some articles will show up next to content that dramatically impacts the credibility of sound reporting. For example, if a story about an election outcome shows up in a newsfeed next to a fake article with conflicting views, this may confuse the reader as to what source to trust.

This risk emerges at the juncture of technology, editorial standards, and strategy. Also on the line is a dramatic change in revenue generation. When considering content syndication, publishers should safeguard their brand from dilution by distributing content to select partners only. However, diversification is equally important, as reliance on a single third-party platform might hinder long-term growth of both audiences and revenue. Most importantly, it's crucial to ensure editorial control over the overall news experience, especially when consumption happens outside the publisher's digital properties.

For most of the twentieth century and at the beginning of the twenty-first, news media companies (whether print, broadcast, or online), generated revenue primarily through subscriptions or other recurring fees and advertising, and the amount of money earned corresponded, at least indirectly, to audience size. With the advent of the internet, earlier this century, publishers increasingly turned to external platforms to build their brands.

Now publishers no longer simply aim to acquire traffic through search and social. They are also syndicating through third-party platforms such as Facebook, Twitter, YouTube, Snapchat, and more. Traffic acquisition strategies have the primary goal of driving readers back to the publisher's own properties, while approaches to content syndication focus on engaging audiences outside the publisher's site and monetizing them through revenue share agreements with third-party platforms.

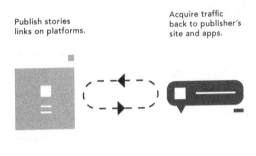

Publish stories links on platforms.

Acquire traffic back to publisher's site and apps.

Publish full story directly on platforms and monetize through revenue share agreements.

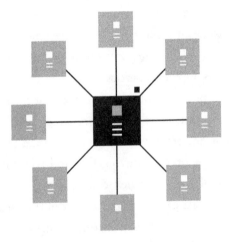

FIGURE 1.7: Traffic acquisition vs. content syndication to third-party platforms.

By talking with industry peers, the Newsmaker identified a few ideas to explore when considering syndicating content.

Not only does this new distribution strategy require new business models; it also requires new ways of thinking on the editorial side. Newsrooms are becoming responsible for multiple platforms, and editors are becoming more than simply journalists—they are now "information officers," who must adapt to different platforms while keeping an eye on the original scope of the story and the framework in which information is gathered.

Media organizations including Reuters, the *Chicago Tribune*, Hearst, and CBS Interactive deploy AI-powered content distribution platform TrueAnthem to determine what stories should be recirculated and when they should be posted across social media platforms.[28] To make these decisions, the system tracks signals that predict performance, including the level of audience engagement, publishing frequency, and time of the day. The platform also automatically generates copy for posts using the tone and voice of the publication by indexing content and extracting descriptive metadata from the articles.

1.3. A NEW MODEL REQUIRES A NEW WAY OF WORKING

Over the years, the Newsmaker's organization has found its budgets shrinking in the face of declining advertising and subscription revenues. The reality is that news organizations are now competing in an oversupplied news market that demands journalists create more with less.

In the midst of all of this rapid change, an email arrives in the Newsmaker's inbox from her editor in chief. It's entitled "The way forward."

Dear colleagues,

In a period of disruption, the best way to anticipate change is to invest in internal capabilities and promote new thinking.

It's crucial to bring everyone into the process of experimentation rather than establishing an independent innovation unit. This organic process starts with "agents of change" within the newsroom.

As such, we are seeking five colleagues to go through a training program focused on research and experimentation best practices.

Participants will then be responsible for bringing that knowledge back to their departments and establishing a culture that encourages new ideas as well as problem solving.

- Editor-in-Chief

The Newsmaker's editor is right. When "innovation agents" are concentrated in a single department, problems will crop up:

- Little or no open communication with other groups in the editorial department or with the product and technology teams

- Too much focus on experimentation, with no real direction or alignment with the overall strategy of the newsroom

- Isolation from important conversations happening elsewhere in the newsroom

This all results in "innovation" projects with limited impact.

LEVERAGING AI IN THE NEWSROOM REQUIRES A NEW PROCESS

Newsmakers throughout the industry are experimenting with and deploying artificial intelligence to alleviate the current straits, but to succeed the change must be organic. Newsroom transformation is not about technology; it's about cultural change. This starts by fostering an environment where journalists are encouraged to pilot, to fail, to get feedback, to iterate. AI accelerates the process of collecting and contextualizing data, which is integral to the overall journalistic process. Deploying these capabilities requires a new way of working that:

- Emphasizes experimentation, including making data-driven decisions to develop new content and build new products

- Fosters collaboration, where the editorial and technology staffs work together to identify new opportunities and address existing challenges

- Looks beyond the industry to find and implement best practices that help teams better understand audiences, new technologies, and generational shifts

This new process is called iterative journalism, which we will explore in detail in chapter 3 of this book.

2

ENABLERS

THE AI TECHNOLOGIES DRIVING
JOURNALISTIC CHANGE

There is no universal definition of artificial intelligence. For computer scientists, AI might look like algorithms capable of thinking like humans. For bioengineers, it might mean growing brain cells in a laboratory. But how should journalists think about AI?

One way of thinking about AI in news organizations is in terms of the interaction between humans and machines and the journalistic results of that collaboration.

2.1. HUMAN-MACHINE
STORYTELLING COLLABORATION

The Newsmaker has been assigned to cover a debate between two politicians. In looking for a new angle that provides a different way for her readers to understand the event, the Newsmaker, in collaboration with her technology team, applies an open-source emotion analysis program to analyze video recordings of a debate between two politicians. The software tracks and analyzes the dominant expressions on the politicians' faces: one is happy when talking about her tax agenda; the other is surprised by a question about his position on the minimum wage. This emotion analysis software can also chart the points and topics in the debate that caused anger, anxiety, and so on.

The Newsmaker's colleagues elsewhere in the newsroom are intrigued by—but also skeptical about—this novel approach.

"How is a computer able to know someone's emotions?" a business reporter asks.

"It's all based on AI algorithms trained to identify micro-expressions," the Newsmaker explains. "The computer identifies multiple points on a face and, based on those points, it's able to calculate the probability of a certain facial expression correlating to a certain emotion—for example, raised eyebrows is correlated to the emotion of surprise."[1]

These types of artificial intelligence programs can give journalists the power to identify patterns and trends from multiple data sources, remotely analyze scenes in the field for objects, faces, and texts, and even better understand tone and sentiment from sources. In the case of political debates, they can offer new insights into which issues candidates actually feel impassioned by beyond the broad issues tied to their campaigns.

For example, the *Wall Street Journal* used sentiment analysis to quantify responses to a survey on polarization in America.[2] Online publication *Quartz* had a computer watch a televised debate between Hillary Clinton and Donald Trump, and recognize dominant emotions measured by facial expressions for each candidate.[3] Although *Quartz* reported that the algorithm found that Clinton was happier when compared to Trump, it also noted that the methodology was still nascent and therefore prone to error.

Convinced by the Newsmaker's explanation, the business reporter decides to apply the same algorithm to analyze the dominant emotions of a CEO announcing her company's financial gains and losses. But the algorithm doesn't find any meaningful correlation between the CEO's emotions and the information she announces during an earnings call. Actually, at times the computer indicates that the executive is sad when she is noticeably happy.

That's because, in order to learn, machines need to be taught.

Algorithms require training data, in this case, hundreds (if not thousands) of photos and videos of that same CEO with different expressions. The AI system needs a series of images that the reporter knows show the CEO when she's happy, and a series of images that the reporter knows show her when she is sad. This is a kind of intuition-building that we all go through, often as children. The machine relies on this data to interpret each new image or video frame of the CEO, because humans express and calibrate their facial movements differently. In this project, the reporter does not provide that training data and is thus unable to determine how the AI is making decisions, leading to inconclusive results.

BASED ON THE TRAINING DATA, HOW WILL THE ALGORITHM LABEL THIS IMAGE?

FIGURE 2.1: The process of creating a machine-learning model relies on providing the algorithm training data to learn from. The training set must include the correct answer, in this case whether an image includes someone who is happy or sad. The system then learns how to find patterns with the goal of correctly labeling new images.

The advanced insights this type of software can provide does not mean they should be implemented in an unregulated process. In addition to accuracy, a secondary concern is that a new set of privacy standards may be necessary, precisely because of the incentive such AI systems gives companies for collecting training data.

In a story highlighting the prevalence of AI surveillance in China, journalists at the *Wall Street Journal* built a facial recognition tool within the article, allowing readers to upload their webcam feed and automatically determine their own emotional state.[4] The project was meant to demonstrate how AI technology works, but also to stress its privacy implications. Before submitting a photo or video for analysis, readers were warned with the following terms of use: "*The Wall Street Journal* is not uploading, storing or broadcasting any of your information in this demo. Video images and photos from your computer appear only on your computer."

At the heart of artificial intelligence is a machine that simplifies complex questions (What does a facial expression mean?) into smaller, more approachable tasks that feed into an output (the CEO is happy, sad, or surprised).

The success of a newsroom still relies on how human journalists implement these new tools, and on the ethical, editorial, and economic considerations grounding their decisions. But more immediately, and on less theoretical terms, AI is transformational insofar as it changes the cost structure for the production of information. Producing content in mass amounts could cost next to zero once the appropriate technology is up and running. The world is moving from a state of information scarcity to one of abundance. When it's so easy and cheap to produce content, it presents both an opportunity and a challenge.

This is where augmentation comes into effect.

FROM AUTOMATION TO AUGMENTATION

The first wave of the collaboration between humans and smart machines has been news automation, where artificial intelligence systems generate alerts and written stories directly from data.

Because of the formulaic nature of certain sports, financial, and economic news, the Newsmaker has the ability to automate some of those stories. But the AI tools still require help from a human, so the Newsmaker needs to write a specific story template for the newsbot to populate. A template for a sports update reads:

> [Team name] *scored* [adjective] [number of points] *in* [quarter], *as* [player] *led the way with* [frequency of scores] [types of scores]

By performing repetitive and laborious functions at scale, AI is helping the Newsmaker's colleagues to engage in more complex, qualitative reporting. In other words, the goal of automation is not to displace journalists from their jobs—it's about freeing up their time from labor-intensive tasks so they can do higher-order journalism. Automated stories about a regular-season baseball game can free sports reporters to pursue more complex pieces, such as examining the long-term impact of concussions in American football or investigating the sex abuse scandal surrounding USA Gymnastics.

Following automation, the next evolution the Newsmaker can experiment with involves smart tools that augment her own reporting. This involves AI-powered interfaces that provide context to topics and can even optimize a news report by means of its dateline and subject matter.

For example, this kind of software helps the Newsmaker by recommending facts and figures about the sources, locations, and organizations she writes about—all in real time. The system searches through an archive of past news articles and quickly finds all instances where someone (or something) has been mentioned, retrieving valuable information that contextualizes her reporting. For instance, in a recent story about a construction company being investigated for fraud, the AI surfaces a list of five previous contracts awarded by the city council totaling millions of dollars. In addition, it reveals the name of a lawyer who has been mentioned in two past reports about the builder. The system shows detailed results as it uncovers relationships among entities including people, organizations, and figures.

These capabilities help the Newsmaker do more investigative work by analyzing massive sets of data and pointing to relationships among data that would be invisible to even the most experienced reporter. The computer handles the numbers, freeing up the journalist to focus on narrative.

The International Consortium of Investigative Journalists (ICIJ) uses an AI-powered tool to automatically recognize and index text documents.[5] This smart software was used by ICIJ reporters to make sense of 13.4 million confidential documents relating to offshore investments, an effort that eventually became an influential journalistic series—"Paradise Papers: Secrets of the Global Elite."

This combination of AI and journalism has the potential to contribute to a more informed society by empowering journalists to conduct deep analysis, uncover corruption, and hold people and institutions accountable—and do all of it much more efficiently than ever before. Eventually, as costs of technology go down, these new tools will prevail in most of the world's newsrooms. AI is becoming much more accessible to journalists, including freelancers and those working in small newsrooms. Rather than investing in developing custom solutions, newsrooms can partner with start-ups. These emerging players are rapidly developing solutions that are easy to use and, most importantly, solve real pain points in the workflow. But we should not expect mass adoption will come about without complications.

AI BRINGS COMPLEXITIES INTO THE NEWSROOM

As smart machines make their way into newsrooms, journalists need to carefully consider how data is used to train algorithms and how smart machines make decisions or draw conclusions.

Replicating human judgment is not an inevitable technological outcome. As it progresses, AI journalism faces the challenge of developing a kind of "journalistic intuition." This is particularly true, for example, with voice analysis, because humans have a very complex and adaptive way of assessing value judgments in one another's speech.

When the Newsmaker speaks with a source, she employs an intrinsic barometer that assesses the relative value of the words the other person is using. She knows that when the coach of Fairview's basketball team, who tends to exaggerate, describes a victory as "astonishing," the word has a different relative value than when somebody who is rarely impressed uses it.

As relationships develop, the human brain gains an increasingly sophisticated understanding of one another's speech patterns. It remains a question whether a machine can develop journalistic intuition through data inputs.

In the United States, a journalist can take footage of people so long as they are in a public space. It might seem that the same privacy rules would apply for cameras that detect human emotion or for any other new data collection systems. But privacy rules and standards are adjusted according to technological advances. These rules will likely change depending on the kinds of data that can be systematically captured and recorded, and as technologies such as image and audio analysis become exponentially more advanced. For example, under the European Union's General Data Protection Regulation (GDPR), residents have a right to be "free from automated decision making" and to know the logic behind decisions made by AI. Under many circumstances, companies must delete subjects' data upon their request.

For this reason, algorithms require the close supervision of journalists as AI-powered tools become increasingly prominent in the production, processing, and distribution of content. Just as it is important to verify a source's reliability, so it is to confirm the reliability of smart machines and the data used to train them. Things are most likely to go wrong not because of faulty technology, but because the logical commands that create the framework for AI are difficult to perfect. AI is created by humans, and humans make mistakes.

Now, computers are not like simple tools. They need to be trained. Taking on the role of a teacher, the Newsmaker nurtures the capabilities of her student (the AI). She encourages it when it does well, and discourages it when it disappoints. To some degree, machines can also manage their own training, through methods like reinforcement learning, where the program determines the balance between learning new things and leveraging what it already knows. However, even in this case, human programmers are needed to oversee and refine the machine's performance.

Journalists can streamline the process of assessing the reliability of algorithms by developing documentation to be used as a reference for future projects.

EXPECT ORGANIZATIONAL PUSHBACK

Despite the proliferation of artificial intelligence in the media industry, most journalists still know very little about the ethical implications of news augmentation by AI. Because it is clear that the integration of these technologies will drastically change various industries and our relationship with information, caution is necessary when extrapolating the benefits to journalism.

In the evolution of successful media technologies, there is always a life cycle in its adoption. The first phase of adoption is uncertainty: when a new media technology begins to enter mainstream society, there's a hesitancy to adopt it.

INFORMATION TO INCLUDE WHEN DOCUMENTING AI PROJECTS IN THE NEWSROOM

- **OVERVIEW:** What AI system is being used and what are its attributes?

- **METHODOLOGY:** Why was this particular algorithm used and how was the data sourced?

- **PROCESS:** What steps were taken to ensure editorial quality and accurate results?

- **EDGE CASES:** What potential errors were flagged with the data and algorithm?

- **DISCLOSURE:** How was the audience informed of the use of AI?

- **NEWSROOM IMPACT:** What were the success metrics in terms of story engagement, differentiation, time savings, etc.?

When the first media technology was introduced—writing on paper—Greek philosopher Socrates argued that "the written word is the enemy of memory."

Centuries later, with the introduction of the printing press, German cryptographer Johannes Trithemius worried that the new technology would make monks, who were responsible for transcribing religious books, lazy.

The world underwent similar resistance to the introduction of the typewriter and even to the word processors in today's computers.

Similar concerns to the ones described above have been raised about AI in recent years. Renowned Harvard law professor Jonathan Zittrain has warned that the "overreliance on artificial intelligence may put us in intellectual debt."[6]

As new technology enters the bloodstream of the media industry, the second phase of adoption occurs. Moving beyond hesitancy, users begin to realize a new technology's potential. A given technology might be wildly beneficial, but this doesn't mean that ignoring any initial critical views and blindly adopting it is a good approach. Any process of adopting new technology should respect tradition even as it embraces innovation.

The transition to augmented journalism, where smart machines help newsrooms create better and faster content, will likely encounter hesitancy to adopt. Journalists need to understand machines enough to know they won't replace them—but it's natural and necessary for them to reserve a dose of skepticism about AI. In fact, many newsroom tools are developed using external, preexisting models from large corporations such as Google, Microsoft, and Amazon, which newsrooms should evaluate thoroughly before using.

For example, a data scientist working at a news organization might build a moderation tool for its comments section that automatically flags bad comments by using a machine learning model developed by Google. Under these circumstances, it is important that the AI is trained using data from the publisher's site—in this case, a historical log of human-moderated comments that have been labeled as "rejected" vs. "accepted."

Smart systems must be audited; their algorithm designs and functions should be evaluated to prevent unforeseen pitfalls. It's crucial to evaluate attributes such as the accuracy of results, speed, and ability to scale across the newsroom. This is yet another consideration for news organizations prior to the scaling of AI in newsrooms: auditing cannot be an afterthought in developing AI. It might be tempting to think that technology must be developed before we think about regulating or "training" it, but smart technologies don't work this way.

Another important consideration for news organizations is related to costs. When tools are developed in-house, the newsroom will have expenses related to data processing and cloud computing that can quickly go up if not properly monitored.

The Newsmaker wisely builds trust with her colleagues by including them in discussions, by sharing research, and by being transparent about the potential technological pitfalls.

Creating frameworks, documentation, and processes for human intervention in AI is crucial to its development and technological advancements in the space. These systems

HOW ARE AI NEWSROOM APPLICATIONS BUILT?

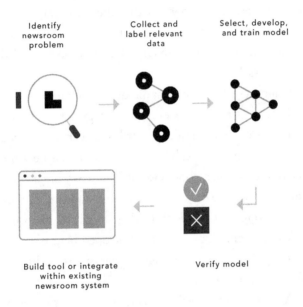

Identify newsroom problem

Collect and label relevant data

Select, develop, and train model

Build tool or integrate within existing newsroom system

Verify model

FIGURE 2.2: The development of artificial intelligence requires constant validation of both the data sources and the algorithms used in that tool.

must be transparent, accountable, and explainable. For example, nonprofit artificial intelligence research organization OpenAI developed an automated news article program that could generate a full article based on just a few keywords. However, the researchers evaluating this program determined that it could easily lend itself to fake news in the hands of bad actors, and so it was decided that the program would not be released to the public.[7] Human considerations of the benefits and costs of technology are crucial to a healthy journalistic ecosystem. Just because technology offers a new capability, it doesn't mean it should be integrated into the newsroom.

It's up to the industry to consider the tradeoffs that the technology presents. At the same time, news organizations should not become paralyzed by the strategic choice of whether and how to adopt AI.

2.2. ARTIFICIAL INTELLIGENCE AND NEWSROOM STRATEGY

The decision to use AI should be informed by whether it can help expand newsrooms' capabilities to increase the volume of stories, produce differentiated journalism, and streamline workflows. When journalists use AI-powered tools to enhance their reporting, research, writing, and editing, it is called augmented journalism.

Some key concerns with AI in the newsroom are machine bias, the risks inherent in unchecked algorithmic news generation, the potential for workflow changes, legal liability, and the growing gap in skill sets required to manage this new specialty area. An automated reporting program incorrectly produced an article in July 2015 saying that the Netflix stock price had fallen by 71 percent when it had, in fact, more than doubled—this was due to a mistaken analysis of the term "7–1" in its data.[8] Poor or incorrect data, or data phrased in unexpected ways, can cause automated reporting programs to put out false facts. Unchecked machine-based data analysis can also lead to biases in reporting, the same types of biases that exist elsewhere in AI applications. These are important areas of consideration that journalists must evaluate, as discussed in previous sections of this book.

In the near future, news organizations will have an arsenal of AI-powered tools at their disposal, and journalists will be able to integrate smart machines into their everyday work. Machine intelligence will be able to do much more than put out straightforward, automated news reports.

Newsrooms should think about AI as a tool that can solve a problem or create an opportunity. From a broad perspective, it can help address issues that would require a lot of repetitive work or a lot of people to do it. Armed with it, newsrooms should ask themselves why, where, and how they will be implementing these smart machines.

Why: Is the news organization using artificial intelligence to systematize or enhance internal workflows? AI can be deployed to scale, lowering the cost of production (automation) and shifting resources toward the creation of tailored, unique content (augmentation).

- Focus on *automation* when a certain task requires a lot of repetitive work or a lot of people to do it. This approach is relevant when the output you are trying to produce does not have to be differentiated.

- Focus on *augmentation* when a human task can be improved through the help of a machine. This is the right choice for complex tasks that require a lot of computational power—for example, analyzing a large dataset of financial data as part of an investigative piece.

Where: Is the goal to generate new content, such as automated reports, or is it to increase efficiency in a process—tagging photos or labeling articles, for example—involving stories already produced?

- *Content* should be automated when news organizations need to serve a big audience, or alternatively to serve an audience that has a very specific interest (usually local journalism). In fact, automation can be leveraged to produce many versions of the same story with slightly different angles (for example, to include localized information). Finally, automation can be deployed to produce content that otherwise would not have been created. Keep in mind that, too much content automation will devalue the overall output of the newsroom.

- *Processes* throughout the newsroom can and should be automated when possible. Applying AI to a certain activity (for example, adding metadata to stories) can dramatically reduce human error and improve the overall uniformity of how content is labeled. This approach is relevant when humans create disparate outputs that in turn impact the overall efficiency of the newsroom.

How: Should news organizations build AI tools using internal capabilities, or partner with a technology company or universities? Third-party tools are becoming better and easier to use, but they may require additional staff training.

- *Build* internally if you have the financial resources to invest in the development and maintenance of the tool, and if the system you are building is not readily available in the market. AI can become an important competitive differentiator, but it also requires substantial capital allocation. Building internally is usually more suitable for large newsrooms that have very specific needs and large budgets.

- *Partner* with a technology provider (or a university) if you don't require custom AI features or capabilities. This is a cost-effective approach for newsrooms with smaller budgets, independent journalists, and freelancers.

SHOULD NEWSROOM BUILD OR PARTNER?

The *Washington Post*'s natural-language-generation tool Heliograph provided the *Post*'s audience with automatically generated daily updates during the 2016 Summer Olympics, using structured datasets (data that is organized by rows and columns) such as results, medal counts, and event schedules.[9] The updates were delivered through social media in the form of text alerts or through Amazon Alexa as voice updates.

But not all news organizations build their own tools. The Associated Press preferred to partner with tech company

CRITERIA TO CONSIDER WHEN EVALUATING WHETHER TO BUILD OR PARTNER

COST:

BUILD

- Building newsroom tools requires hiring a technical staff member with engineering, data science, and design expertise. There are also additional costs associated with web servers and data storage.

PARTNER

- Third-party start-ups usually charge a monthly fee, which could range from a couple of hundred dollars to thousands, depending on usage or number of accounts. Using external technology is the most efficient way for independent journalists or freelancers to start implementing AI in their workflow.

STABILITY:

BUILD

- Developing a tool internally will require conducting regular maintenance on the software and addressing system errors.

PARTNER

- A third-party provider will have tested their tools with dozens of other clients and is constantly updating its functionality.

CONTINUED

CUSTOMIZATION:

BUILD

- Creating a tool internally allows for a newsroom to tailor a solution to the specific needs of its journalists and their workflows.

PARTNER

- A tool from a partner is usually a more generalized solution, applicable to different companies across industries.

PRIVACY:

BUILD

- Journalists might be more comfortable analyzing proprietary data or confidential documents using internal tools, knowing that no one outside the organization will have access to it.

PARTNER

- Partners' tools may not be any less secure than internal ones, but there's always an issue of perception.

Automated Insights when it came to automating sports stories, while the UK's Press Association collaborated with tech platform Arria.

For smaller news organizations or independent journalists, it is generally advisable to get started by testing several partner tools before proceeding to build one's own tools.

2.3. THE TECHNOLOGIES SHAPING THE NEW MODEL OF JOURNALISM

Artificial intelligence encompasses several subdomains that can improve human storytelling in modern newsrooms.

Machine learning (ML) simplifies complex ideas into smaller, more approachable tasks that ultimately lead to a designated end point. There are three main types: "supervised," "unsupervised," and "reinforcement learning." These ML paradigms help reporters draw conclusions from large corpora of data.

USING SUPERVISED LEARNING TO FIND A LINK BETWEEN A KNOWN INPUT AND A KNOWN OUTPUT

Thanks to several anonymous tips, the Newsmaker and her colleagues suspect there are irregularities in campaign financing for a certain state senator. However, they can't afford to allocate human resources from the newsroom to investigate the campaign. The tips are highly speculative, but, if true, would point to a hugely consequential story.

This is where machine learning enters the picture. The team could use supervised learning to train an algorithm to analyze thousands of financial documents from past campaigns that were convicted of illegal financing activity or that bypassed federal contribution limits. The system learns what items those documents have in common—names of corporations or unions banned from donating money directly to candidates, for example—and determines a correlation between the characteristics in the documents and the political campaign in question.

In the case of the state senator, there is a known input (financing documents) and a known, or, for now, suspected output (that those documents have irregularities). The team feeds the financial documents belonging to the suspected campaign through the system and allows the AI to determine whether the business is likely to be receiving illegal financing.

Machine learning relies mostly on algorithms—a set of dynamic rules that, when followed, lead to the desired solution. Based on historical data, a machine can flag points of interest in new data. So, given the campaign financing documents, the software might suggest that if a candidate has received over $2 million in under one month with more than seven unnamed sources, there is an 80 percent chance of illegal activity.

It's correlation, not causation, but an 80 percent probability based on historical data is enough to flag a scenario for deeper journalistic investigation. There are no conclusions here yet, though, just an early observation.

Using machine learning, the *Atlanta Journal-Constitution* uncovered sex abuse by doctors, as recounted in a series of 2016 stories on how physicians were able to keep their licenses after being disciplined.[10] A data journalist for the paper scraped regulators' websites to collect complaints to medical boards (the agencies that license doctors) across fifty states. The reporter then used machine learning to analyze one hundred thousand disciplinary documents based on keywords and to allocate a probability score of a case being related to sexual misconduct by a doctor. These data insights were then used by the reporter to guide the journalistic investigation, by narrowing down which hospitals to focus on and which sources to pursue.

ALGORITHMS MAKE MISTAKES

Constructing machine learning algorithms is exceptionally difficult, and the results of a poorly constructed one can be catastrophic, not only for journalists developing stories but also when media organizations rely on them to determine how and what news stories should be distributed to readers.

The two most common errors in machine learning are, using terms we borrow from statisticians, type I (false negative) and type II (false positive) errors.

A false negative would mean that the algorithm used by the Newsmaker has classified an illegal financing item as legal. Needless to say, the Newsmaker doesn't want that. This error might occur due to multiple factors, including the documents used to train the algorithm not being properly labeled by humans. A false positive would mean that her algorithm has classified a legal financing document as illegal. She doesn't want that, either.

FIGURE 2.3: The two most common errors in machine learning are false negatives and false positives.

What the Newsmaker wants is a system that can, with a high level of accuracy, label illegal financing as illegal, and law-abiding campaign funds as not being illegal.

Again, her colleagues ask: How?

"We use campaign financing data to teach our algorithm," the Newsmaker responds. "Algorithms are written by humans, and humans make errors. Therefore, our AI machine may well make an error, especially in its early stages."

The Newsmaker raises an important issue here. It's the responsibility of modern journalists to know what their systems are doing and to be confident in what they are publishing. Understanding the nature of the AI as well as the data flowing through it can provide newsrooms insight into potential algorithmic errors. In fact, there's an editorial decision to be made. No system is going to be 100 percent accurate, so which would the Newsmaker rather tend toward, false positives or false negatives? The answer to this question depends on the type of journalistic work being developed and should be evaluated on a case by case basis.

UNSUPERVISED LEARNING: WHEN THE NEWSMAKER DOESN'T KNOW WHAT TO LOOK FOR

The Newsmaker is looking for possible story lines for an interesting business feature on the effect of a new Fairview marijuana dispensary on nearby retail. This is an issue that has been dividing the local community for over a year. In fact, many community members have voiced their concern that selling cannabis products will increase crime and negatively impact the surrounding area.

The Newsmaker instructs the smart system to take all of the data she collected—number of new business licenses, hours of operation of different businesses, reported incidents of shoplifting, and more—as the input and to discover possible patterns.

The system finds that restaurants within a three-mile radius of the dispensary have increased sales and hired more people compared to those that are further way; and that shoplifting is more likely to occur on Sunday evenings (when the dispensary happens to be closed).

The computer isn't looking for anything in particular, but it might still surface something worth reporting on.

Unlike supervised learning, unsupervised learning is given no target output. The system has free rein to derive relationships between input and output, usually by comparing similarities and deviations across data points. Some of these approaches will require a journalist to partner with a technologist on staff. For smaller newsrooms and freelancers who may not have such resources, a possible solution is to collaborate with academic researchers with an interest in the topic.

Machine learning is a powerful tool that allows humans to see things they otherwise could not when datasets get above a certain size.

Take sports data. Sports fans are often interested in obscure statistics and numerical correlations. An unsupervised learning machine can look, for example, at basketball statistics over the course of the season and alert journalists when unusual correlations are taking place. The machine could alert the journalist (without them ever having asked for the information) that four players have drastically increased their offensive efficiency in the past month while playing fewer minutes. This could form the basis of a story.

REINFORCEMENT LEARNING: OPTIMIZING PUBLISHING

The other major type of machine learning is "reinforcement learning." Here, the machine teaches itself by exploring its environment—and this type of learning has in fact often been used to train self-driving cars and to play complex board games on a computer such as chess and Go. In journalism it has been deployed to build out interactive features where audiences can engage with programs to learn more about AI itself. For example, the *New York Times* ran a dynamic graphic where a program trained on reinforcement learning battles users in a game of rock-paper-scissors to accompany an article about game-playing AI.[11]

The deployment of these algorithms is still nascent when it comes to developing a story. However, reinforcement learning can also be applied to optimize publishing; for example, to help choose the best headlines or thumbnails for a particular story. In 2016, Microsoft used a type of reinforcement learning called contextual bandits to select optimal headlines for MSN.com, improving click-through rates by 25 percent.[12] This system functions as a more sophisticated form of A/B testing. It assesses the context (e.g., the time of day that a reader visits the site, the device used, their region), takes an action (e.g., what headline to display), and observes the outcome of that decision (e.g., did the user click on the story or not). Each outcome is associated with a reward. Reinforcement learning works by maximizing the average reward.

Another emerging approach in machine learning is called "deep learning," which focuses on teaching machines to learn more complex types of data representations, such as images or long sections of text, by increasing the complexity of the program and minimizing the "loss function"—a measure of how good a model does in terms of being able to predict a certain outcome.

Deep learning can be supervised or unsupervised or somewhere in between. It has been used to complete sophisticated generative tasks, such as creating cover art for an issue of *Bloomberg Businessweek* on AI.[13] These tasks are typically done using neural networks, which are advanced computing systems inspired by biological neural networks, in the brain. This type of AI has other potential applications to journalism, particularly when it comes to research. The Newsmaker is using it to analyze complex legal documents, because the AI is able to automatically translate technical terminology into simple language that someone with no legal expertise is able to understand. Neural networks imitate how humans learn and process information: the machine "reads" many documents and tries to identify specific patterns. For example, it realizes that every time "class action" is mentioned, the concept of "lawsuit" is associated with a "group of people" (as opposed to a specific individual).

NEWS AUTOMATION

When the Newsmaker needs to generate content automatically, she turns to natural language algorithms that can comprehend and analyze how humans communicate. She has learned that there are two important fields of AI related to natural language: natural language generation and natural language processing.

Natural language generation (NLG) enables the automation of repetitive tasks like writing news articles that follow a well-defined structure. The Newsmaker recently obtained access to the following real estate data set.

TOWN	HOME SALES (THIS YEAR)	HOME SALES (LAST YEAR)
FAIRVIEW	1400	1500
SPRINGFIELD	1100	1000
FRANKLIN	800	800

FIGURE 2.4: Many natural language generation systems used by newsrooms require structured data, organized in rows and columns.

She can use this to test an NLG tool that enables her to write templates and automatically create text outputs directly from structured data, here organized in rows and columns. She decides to develop the following story template:

> Home sales in [town] measured [home sales this
> year] this year, [a decline / an increase /
> staying flat] compared to [home sales last
> year] sales recorded last year.

This example is only the most basic, where the bracketed words represent interchangeable data points within a specific variable. Many other time-consuming tasks, like earnings reports, sports recaps, and economic indicator updates, can also be automated.

Using this methodology to automate part of its financial coverage, the Associated Press went from covering 300 companies with human writers to covering over 4,400 companies with machines, a nearly fifteen-fold increase. Using the same methodology, the Norwegian News Agency is able to generate a soccer report thirty seconds after the match has ended.

BRANCH WRITING: THINKING THROUGH VARIATIONS

The function of writing templates is commonly referred to as "branch writing," because the story can have multiple variations. Branch writing means telling the natural language generation system to write a certain word or sentence under a particular condition; like in computer programming, it's an if-then-else logic.

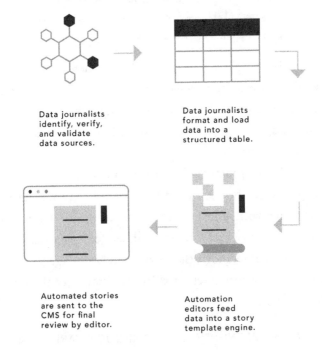

Data journalists
identify, verify,
and validate
data sources.

Data journalists
format and load
data into a
structured table.

Automated stories
are sent to the
CMS for final
review by editor.

Automation
editors feed
data into a story
template engine.

FIGURE 2.5: Human journalists have a crucial role at every step of data–to–text automation process.

For the story template example cited above, the Newsmaker creates the following condition:

- **CONDITION 1:** If [home sales this year] < [home sales last year], then write [a decline].

- **CONDITION 2:** If [home sales this year] > [home sales last year], then write [an increase].

- **CONDITION 3:** If [home sales this year] = [home sales last year], then write [staying flat].

The Newsmaker uses the tool to input the data into the template that matches the conditions. With the click of a button, she generates the following three alerts:

STORY FROM CONDITION 1:

Home sales in **Fairview** *measured* **1,400** *this year, a* **decline** *compared to* **1,500** *sales recorded last year.*

STORY FROM CONDITION 2:

Home sales in **Springfield** *measured* **1,100** *this year, an* **increase** *compared to* **1,000** *sales recorded last year.*

STORY FROM CONDITION 3:

Home sales in **Franklin** *measured* **800** *this year,* **staying flat** *compared to* **800** *sales recorded last year.*

STRUCTURE   TEMPLATE   AUTOMATION

FIGURE 2.6: The process of data text generation requires journalists to write story templates.

Although branch writing remains the predominant approach to text automation in the news industry, there are emerging natural language tools that are able to learn the structure of a given story and automatically generate a template. In this case, the editor does not have to create a template from scratch, but merely to review the output for quality.

Programs that create automated reports using structured datasets can help journalists generate hundreds of stories. But when so many stories are generated using the same templates, there's a risk of those reports becoming too repetitive. To address the issue, many NLG systems used by newsrooms, including Automated Insights and Arria, allow journalists like the Newsmaker to replace words with synonyms to differentiate each piece of content.

Home sales in Fairview **measured** 1,400 this year, a decline **compared** to 1,500 sales **recorded last year**.

Or

Real estate sales in Springfield **reached** 1,100 this year, an increase **in comparison** to 1,000 sales **registered in the year prior**.

CASE STUDY: *LE MONDE'S* AUTOMATION OF ELECTIONS

In 2015, the French newspaper *Le Monde* partnered with AI company Syllabs to cover local elections.[14] In the weeks leading up to the election, the publication connected Syllabs news-writing algorithms to open data sets from the French National Institute of Statistics and Economic Studies and the ministry of the interior to preview results from each of the 34,000 municipalities.[15] These stories included data such as rates of local economic growth, unemployment, and inflation. The project also helped the bots learn the editorial style of *Le Monde*, in advance of the elections. As the votes came in on the night of the election, these bots produced news articles on results for every municipality. This freed up time for *Le Monde's* human reporters to produce in-depth articles analyzing the significance of each election. The automated stories significantly boosted *Le Monde's* search engine optimization traffic by having more published stories online, allowing them to beat out competitor France TV Info by almost three hundred thousand unique visitors.

AUTOMATION EDITORS JOIN THE NEWSROOM

After testing several automation tools, the Newsmaker realizes that there are many high-quality natural language generation providers available, including Automated Insights, Narrative Science, Arria, and Yseop, among others.

In each case, the NLG software gives journalists the ability to create templates and to automate certain tasks. In addition to pricing, an important feature to consider when evaluating what service to use is ease of integration with other tools and data sources. For example, some of these tools allow direct integration with data visualization services such as Tableau and Power BI, which may be relevant to freelance journalists who want to include charts in their automated stories.

This new form of reporting requires thinking through possible variations of the article at both the sentence and word levels. It relies on smart logic and conditions, very different from the inverted pyramid approach (where the most important information is presented first, followed by secondary facts) that the Newsmaker learned in journalism school.

The Newsmaker initiates the process by uploading a spreadsheet containing structured data about the financial results of one hundred publicly traded companies. The tool transforms the columns and rows into variables, which can then be linked to specific fields in the template.

She then directs the system to generate specific sentences under a set of criteria. For example, in one part of the template, she will command the software to write "the company registered profits" only if the value in the spreadsheet cell containing the company's revenue is bigger than the value in the cell for its expenses. She asks the software to write "the company registered losses" if the losses are higher than revenues.

After reviewing some of the stories, she quickly realizes that she did not tell the tool what to write if losses

PRINCIPLES TO KEEP IN MIND WHEN DEPLOYING NATURAL LANGUAGE GENERATION

- Start the process by manually writing a sample story you wish to automate, before trying to create a template.

- Where possible, use similarly structured logic in different branches, to make the process easier and more

- Add synonyms once the core template is ready, in order to avoid duplicating phrasing.

- Consult your newsroom's style guide to ensure references to numbers in are in the proper form (e.g., spelling out "percent" vs. using the symbol %).

- Identify the edge cases that could be problematic to the dataset's logic early in the process instead of responding to them at a later stage.

equal revenues—a third possible option when generating stories about the financial results of these companies. The Newsmaker understands that human journalists should be in control of the automation process. Not only must they write templates and think through possible variations of the story (branches), they must, even more importantly, identify, verify, and validate data sources.

Automated stories need to go through the same editorial standards and processes as human-written content. In the automation process, the journalist is also responsible for ensuring alignment with the newsroom style guide. This includes making sure that the spelling of certain names, titles, numbers, and figures is the same as in any other story published.

A general rule for ensuring a template's quality is to evaluate a subset of stories that contain an example of each core variation. For example, a simple template on home sales across hundreds of cities could have three outputs:

1. Stories about an increase in sales

2. Stories about a decrease in sales

3. Stories about a stagnant market (no increase or decrease)

By evaluating a story for each example, journalists can quickly develop a good sense of potential issues related to each outcome and quickly address them by fixing the template.

Once templates are thoroughly vetted, the focus shifts to evaluating the quality of the data. There's a lower risk for error when the raw input comes from trusted sources, such as a financial data wire or government institutions, or is directly collected by the news organization. However, it is not always possible to draw on such data; it also happens that a given source may become less reliable over time. Like in any other journalistic endeavor, it's crucial to probe the original source and to regularly check what output is being produced.

In fact, journalists should always be on the lookout for potential errors. For instance, a *Los Angeles Times*'s bot in 2017 mistakenly published an automated news update about a 6.8 magnitude earthquake off the coast of California—that actually happened in 1925.[16] The inaccuracy was linked to an error in the United States Geological Survey data and is an important reminder that automated systems require human oversight, such as review from automation editors in the newsroom.

In some instances, an automated story might not provide enough context to a certain news event. For example, a story about the number of houses sold in Fairview might show a drastic drop in sales without explaining that local regulators increased property tax in the area—an important insight that would not have been surfaced in a purely machine-driven story as described above. In such instances, the automation editor is responsible for ensuring that additional information is shared with the reader. In this case, the automation editor may decide to include data—from government sources or other third parties—about the economic impact of the new taxation measure.

False information published through automated production practices could, in some cases, expose the news organization to a libel suit. For this content to be considered defamation, the plaintiff must prove "actual malice" and that the AI was created with the intent of producing false stories. Although no respectable newsroom would never purposely produce misleading news, automation editors must implement human review policies to mitigate such risks. One of the aims of such policies is to ensure that the newsroom owns the rights to the data and that the organization is legally allowed to process and distribute it across channels.

EMERGING NEWSROOM ROLES

The implementation of many newsroom automation and AI processes requires significant human labor.[17] As AI enters the newsroom, the tasks of creating and managing these tools will also change the makeup of the newsroom skillset. In the future, we will see more newsrooms asking for writers that understand how to work with AI, editors that understand how to oversee smart tools, programmers that can design journalistic computer programs, and designers who can evaluate the user experience of reading AI-generated content. In this sense, AIs are not replacing journalistic tasks but augmenting them with roles such as

- **AUTOMATION EDITORS:** responsible for streamlining editorial tasks through AI and ensuring its editorial reliability. They manage the implementation of content automation processes and work across news desks and engineering teams to seamlessly integrate automated stories into internal systems. Automation editors usually have a background in both journalism and computer science.

- **COMPUTATIONAL JOURNALISTS:** responsible for leveraging data science methods to run sophisticated analyses and conduct investigations. They proactively identify opportunities for collaboration with reporters who may not have technical skills but have domain expertise in a specific area of coverage.

- **NEWSROOM TOOL MANAGERS:** responsible for coordinating the implementation of new tools and training journalists how to deploy them. They help the newsroom keep a finger on the pulse of storytelling trends, technologies, and platforms, and continuously evaluate the usefulness of these developments for journalists across the organization.

- **AI ETHICS EDITORS:** responsible for the transparency and explainability of algorithms, as well as the use of training data. They also develop best practices for methodological disclosure and for quickly addressing any issues related to algorithmic errors or bias.

While some newsrooms may hire new personnel to fill these roles, others may instead decide to integrate the key responsibilities into existing roles. For example, the standards and ethics editor may start looking into issues related to algorithmic transparency, while the planning editor might become responsible for promoting the adoption of new tools.

CASE STUDY: USING NATURAL LANGUAGE GENERATION TO LOCALIZE STORIES

The UK's Press Association (PA) uses natural language generation to produce local stories at scale. It even formed a new company, RADAR, to scale production of automated journalism. Articles include trends based on data from the Office for National Statistics, the National Health Service, and other open databases. A local story headline for the borough of Havering, in London, reads, "More than a quarter of Havering children are obese by the end of primary school, says Public Health England." The PA journalists have developed templates for particular topics and use automation to create multiple variations of the same story, each with a unique local angle. In some instances, PA will provide additional context to the data-driven story by adding perspective from human sources.

Statistics from Public Health England show that 23% of Year 6 pupils were declared obese, between April 2016 and March 2017, and 5.3% severely obese.

On top of that 16.1% of Year 6 children were declared overweight.

That means on average 44% of Havering's youngsters are unhealthily overweight when they start secondary school.

And despite school meals getting healthier the number of obese 10- and 11-year-olds in Year 6 has risen by 25% over the last five years.

The figures are from Public Health England's National Child Measurement Programme.

Each year it measures the height and weight of more than one *million children, aged between four and five and 10 and 11, to assess childhood obesity.*

Published in October 2016, Havering Council's Prevention of Obesity Strategy 2016–2019 bases its strategy around three key areas: Shaping the environment to promote healthy eating, supporting a culture that sees physical activity and healthy eating as the norm, and prompting individuals to change, primarily through self-help.

The council also established a permanent subgroup of the Health and Wellbeing Board two years ago to focus solely on tackling obesity.

In the foreword to the council's strategy document, Councillor Wendy Price Thompson insisted everyone involved was working hard to "bring the obesity epidemic under control."

She said: "Austerity isn't a reason for doing nothing—it makes the case for action all the more persuasive.

"The solution isn't investment in new specialist services.

"Rather everyone must do their bit, every day, in terms of the decisions they make, the advice they give, and the actions they take to promote healthy eating and greater physical activity."

Caroline Cerny, lead for the Obesity Health Alliance, a coalition of more than 40 organisations that have joined together to prevent obesity related ill health, described the figures as "startling."

She added: "We've seen a certain amount of progress from government, including the implementation of the soft drinks levy from April this year. But far more needs to be done."[18]

This story is an example of how a local reporter can take an automated draft for their area and further localize it by adding a response or local background information. In this case, the first six paragraphs were automated by RADAR. The reporters for the *Romford Recorder* (where the story was published) added the copy about their local council's (Havering Borough) strategy document. The final two paragraphs were based on an interview with the Obesity Health Alliance.

Across the Atlantic, in San Francisco, the local journalism organization Hoodline uses a similar approach to automatically produce thousands of neighborhood-level stories on restaurant openings and real estate listings by sourcing data from private companies like Yelp as well as open data sources from city governments. A sample Hoodline automated story headline might read something like "Craving Japanese? Check Out These 3 New Philadelphia Spots."[19]

Here's the description for the first restaurant:

As its name indicates, Megumi Japanese Ramen & Sushi Bar is a Japanese spot that specializes in sushi and ramen dishes. It recently debuted in Chinatown. On the ramen menu, look for options like the shoyu pork ramen with a house-made soy sauce and pork broth, miso pork or chicken ramen with bean sprouts, and a spicy chicken ramen with black mushrooms and egg. For lighter fare, the sushi menu offers several different types of rolls, including the "Passion Roll" with lobster salad, spicy tuna, mango, and avocado; and the "Ocean Roll" with salmon, tuna, yellowtail, cucumber, avocado and tobiko. Yelp users are excited about Megumi Japanese Ramen & Sushi Bar, which currently holds 4.5 stars out of 35 reviews on the site. Yelper Joyce S., who reviewed Megumi Japanese Ramen & Sushi Bar on January 12th, wrote: "This is one of my favorite ramen spots. The servers there were friendly and even though they were really busy, they still attended to us when they could. Their ramen is not too salty at all." And Nancy C. said: "Our food arrived within 10 minutes, and the portions were very generous. The noodles were cooked perfectly, and the broth was very flavorful without being too salty. Both bowls of ramen also included half a soft-boiled egg at no additional cost!" Megumi Japanese Ramen & Sushi Bar is open Friday and Saturday from 11am–11pm, and Sunday–Thursday from 11am–10pm.

And here's a second description. Notice the similarity in the story structure as well as the data points used, such as menu descriptions and Yelp reviews.

Tuna Bar recently debuted in Old City. The modern sushi spot offers Japanese flavors with hints of Chinese and Korean influences. It comes courtesy of restaurateurs Ken Sze and Cortney Cohen-

Sze, the couple that is also behind Geisha House. Diners can start with appetizers like tuna crudo with white truffle oil, sashimi salad with wasabi yuzu dressing, and creamy rock shrimp with sweet chili and gochujang. On the sushi menu, expect rolls like the "Old City," with spicy tuna, asparagus, and crispy rock shrimp; the peppered tuna with daikon and wasabi aioli; and a range of nigiri and sashimi. With a five-star rating out of 46 reviews on Yelp, Tuna Bar has been getting positive attention. Yelper Alyssa S., who reviewed Tuna Bar on January 20th, wrote: "They have the most creative sushi I've ever had. Start to finish, from the wine to dessert, everything was amazing. Wine list is solid, and the cocktails looked really interesting." Ben E. noted: "Five stars all around! The sushi here is amazing. The quality and the taste are superb! Not to mention, it's a good looking restaurant with some pretty cool decor and a great ambiance." Tuna Bar is open Friday and Saturday from 5pm–11pm, and Sunday–Thursday from 5pm–10pm.

WHO SHOULD GET THE BYLINE?

If these templates are written by journalists, but the NLG system is the one assembling the final output, the question arises: Who should get credit—the human or the machine?

This question is far from being resolved. A study on the authorship of automated journalism found major differences in crediting policies across twelve news websites.[20]

Editors at the Associated Press, an early adopter of natural language generation, believe that the public should be aware of the machine behind the process. At the bottom of every automated news story, the AP discloses that the story was generated automatically. For example, the following note is included in automated earnings reports:

> This story was generated by Automated Insights [an NLG software provider] using data from Zacks Investment Research [financial data source].

When AP journalists add additional context to an automated story, the corresponding note reads:

> *Portions of this story were generated by Automated Insights using data from Zacks Investment Research.*

At the *Guardian*, automated stories are marked with the following disclaimer:

> *This story was generated by ReporterMate, an experimental automated news reporting system.*

In both cases, the byline goes to the robot.

Meanwhile, automation editors at the Press Association and RADAR felt there was no need to provide credit to the machine, since each story is initiated and crafted by a human reporter who writes the template.

A third model has been implemented by the *Wall Street Journal*, in which both the editor and the automation process are acknowledged. For example, in a project using natural language to create descriptions for nearly 1,000 universities, the *Journal* included the following note in the methodology box:

> *These articles were created with Automated Insights using a template developed by Kevin McAllister and Francesco Marconi of The Wall Street Journal and college rankings data from WSJ/THE.*
>
> *Explore the full methodology and data source list for this year's Wall Street Journal/Times Higher Education College Rankings here [link to full methodology page].*

In the case of the *Journal*, we decided to not only disclose how the stories were developed but also explain the methodology behind the data collection process.

As news automation becomes common practice, newsrooms may argue that these disclosures are no longer needed. But as with any other content with data at its core, it will be important to explain the approach in a way that audiences fully understand. A comparable example is polling stories, which typically include notes on margin of error, population size, and other statistical pitfalls.

But how do readers perceive automated news compared to stories drafted by human journalists? A study conducted by German researchers Mario Haim and Andreas Graefe suggests that while participants considered human-written news easier to read, they preferred automated news for credibility.[21]

NATURAL LANGUAGE PROCESSING: UNDERSTANDING THE COMPLEXITIES OF TEXT

The Newsmaker recently gained access to a comprehensive movie database, with hundreds of thousands of documents containing the names of actors, their biographical information, the films and shows they starred in, their salaries, revenues, and more.

Her editor asked her if there's a way of quickly sifting through the information to find relationships between an actor's background and box office revenues.

Natural language processing (NLP), a sub-domain of AI first developed in the 1950s, can come in handy in these situations. NLP is able to recognize the structure of sentences, understand the semantics of text, and identify people, places, organizations, and concepts in documents. Using NLP, the Newsmaker quickly identifies a trend. Films starring American lead actors (people) who were born on the East Coast (places) generate on average 18 percent more revenue (figures) compared to actors who were born elsewhere.

As in this example, NLP expedites the processes of analyzing correlations among entities, gathering insights, and even fact-checking. This technology is becoming increasingly useful as news organizations try to synthesize information at scale.

- Online publication *Vox* ran this type of text analysis in order to compare eight State of the Union addresses by former President Obama.[22] By quantifying the frequency of terms such as "economy," "jobs," and "war," the analysis identified the most common themes for each year. NLP-based analysis of State of the Union speeches has also been used by the *National Post*, the *New York Times*, and *FiveThirtyEight*.[23]

- The *Wall Street Journal* analyzed the shareholder letter portion of GE's annual report with the goal of understanding the language used by its current and two previous three CEOs.[24] Through this approach, journalists were able to identify (and quantify) catchphrases favored by each of the executives who led the industrial conglomerate. For example, the term "additive manufacturing" (3D printing) was mentioned seven times by Jeff Immelt in 2017, but only four times by his successors in the two years after he stepped down—possibly suggesting a shift in strategic priorities.

- Another business publication, *Quartz*, applied a similar methodology to evaluate car sharing company Lyft's initial public offering filings.[25] In both cases, looking at reoccurrences of terms gave reporters insight into the issues companies care about.

- NLP was used to identify trends in large document troves as part of *Newsday*'s investigation into police misconduct.[26] Reporters used text mining tools to look at 1,700 bills passed in New York State to understand how frequently the legislature had passed police oversight laws.

- In a story for the Associated Press, data journalist Jonathan Stray used text analysis tools to comb through 4,500 declassified documents related to private security contracts in Iraq. This culminated in a story about why and when the U.S. hired these private contractors.[27]

Natural language processing can also be leveraged to create workflow efficiencies. For instance, Hearst Newspapers, which publishes thousands of articles a day across more than thirty local properties, such as the *San Francisco Chronicle* and the *Albany Times Union*, uses NLP to automatically add metadata to its output and save editors' time previously spent doing so.

Finally, NLP technology is helping newsrooms with automated summarization. For example, Bloomberg launched *The Bulletin*, a feature on its mobile app powered by machine-generated summaries that provide readers a "sense of completion in quickly learning the latest news of the moment, and a comprehensive summary of the news that goes beyond a headline."[28]

Natural language processing is also being tested for text personalization and language translation. But NLP is no magic bullet. Text personalization can replicate a particular tone, writing style, and even a political stance; it is increasingly used by marketing agencies to generate content that resonates with a particular individual or demographic, but journalists should give the approach careful consideration before applying it. The impact of text personalization in news raises important ethical issues, as too much personalization will inevitably create information bubbles and fuel a polarization of views.

Language translation using NLP also comes with its own set of problems. The Newsmaker learned this firsthand when she tried to automatically translate an English-language story to Spanish, and the editor of the Spanish section complained about the quality of the translation. The system had trouble interpreting cultural idioms as well as the particular writing style favored by her publication. That's because she was using a standard translation service, which had not been trained on her content. When optimizing an AI model, it is crucial to feed it the right data set: the more specific to the use case, the better. In fact, the Newsmaker could improve the system's ability with idioms by feeding it a host of English and Spanish stories as training data. She would then need to manually tell the NLP what it should and shouldn't do with the more complex sentences.

CASE STUDY: UNDERSTANDING THE USE OF LANGUAGE BY NEWS MEDIA

Following the October 2017 mass shooting in Las Vegas, which left 58 people dead and 851 injured, the debate over media bias in the portrayal of perpetrators of violence according to race and ethnicity was at its peak. Working with a data scientist from Columbia University, *Quartz* used NLP algorithms to analyze 141 hours of major cable news coverage of mass shootings in the immediate two-day period after the news from Las Vegas broke.[29] The software examined transcripts for any correlation between the use of language in the description of specific incidents and the perpetrator's race. One of its findings was that some terms were attached to certain perpetrators more than others, depending on their race or ethnicity—for example, "radical" was mentioned much more frequently in accounts of incidents in which the shooter was identified as nonwhite. Furthermore, for all the twenty-seven mass shooting incidents analyzed, the AI found that news coverage was more likely to mention family members of the shooters if the suspects were identified as white.

SPEECH: ACCESSING INFORMATION THROUGH VOICE

AI helps both with newsgathering and with delivering curated news more efficiently on new platforms. Speech systems provide an example of the latter: they understand the spoken word, distribute content to new platforms, and can help with time-consuming tasks like transcription.

In the internet's "point-and-click" phase desktop websites flourished, but today the internet has entered a "touch" phase dominated by mobile devices and apps that require touch interaction. Voice commands are now ushering us into a third phase, through the "internet of things" and all types of connected devices and experiences. These voice commands carry the potential to link fragmented on-demand experiences, giving audiences the freedom to choose content and consume it across platforms including smart home appliances, voice assistants, and in connected cars. According to a survey by the Reuters Institute for the Study of Journalism, 78 percent of respondents (including forty editors in chief, thirty CEOs or managing editors, and thirty heads of digital at leading traditional media organizations) believe "voice will change how media is accessed over the next few years."[30]

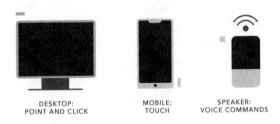

DESKTOP: MOBILE: SPEAKER:
POINT AND CLICK   TOUCH   VOICE COMMANDS

FIGURE 2.7: The devices people use impact how they consume information and how content is published.

These devices rely on AI speech technology. Smart speakers such as Amazon's Alexa or Google Home process a user's voice and convert the audio recording into a set of commands. When the system needs to make sense of questions like "What are the latest headlines?" or "What's the score of the basketball game?," that requires natural language, which is driven by both definitions and relationships between words.

To deliver a response, a smart device needs to analyze the words in a question; retrieve the right answer from a specific data set, such as a news archive or feed (like weather forecasts or sports scores); and, finally, utilize text-to-speech technology to speak back to the user.

This technology is being used by publishers to deliver different types of audio content, including CNN's flash briefings (quick updates on the latest news), the *Washington Post*'s news quizzes on current events, and Hearst's recipes and lifestyle advice. According to a 2019 study conducted by the research firm Voicebot, 13.4 percent of users use smart assistants daily to listen to the news or sports.[31]

Beyond smart speakers, news organizations such as Bloomberg provide automated audio versions of each story through an audio player embedded in each online article. This approach enables publishers to engage consumers who may want to listen to the news using their desktop or mobile phone.

Although there has been progress in the field of speech technology, an important question persists: If an AI system is able to automatically extract facts from multiple news sources and aggregate it into a completely new format, as a voice update, who owns the rights to that content?

Tech giants may ingest news articles on the web to develop their own single-topic news databases. These platforms could, for instance, extract and categorize politicians' signature issues and policy positions and deliver that information on demand without compensating the originators of that information. In the AI internet age, publishers could experience the reemergence of concerns related to fair use and content misappropriation.

TEXT TO SPEECH: OPTIMIZING SPOKEN NEWS

In the same way that publishers have optimized their content for search engines and social networks, they will also need to develop strategies for how their content will play on smart devices.

There are three specific practices that can aid news-rooms in this optimization: structuring data, providing context to the machines through news taxonomies, and improving pronunciation guides and writing style. These practices are particularly relevant to editors responsible for defining content distribution strategies.

1. **STRUCTURED DATA:** Developing a structured news feed or internal knowledge database show-ing relationships between entities (people, places, dates, organizations) mentioned in stories means creating a database categorized across all areas of coverage. This can be accomplished through enti-ty extractions tasks, which refers to bucketing text into predefined categories, such as subject matter or writing style, and through topic modeling, a text analysis method that helps uncover the topics dis-cussed within a piece of text. Both these processes can be used to turn an unorganized archive of news articles into an organized system that can be more easily used by voice devices.

2. **NEWS TAXONOMY:** A news taxonomy is a way of categorizing an article or a certain piece of news. Simply put, it involves adding tags to content. These can be labels related to the type of news (politics, sports), the people or organizations involved (the president of France, the United Nations), or themes (fiscal policy, soccer's World Cup). But beyond those core types of tagging, taxonomies are also currently being developed to indicate what context the news should be consumed in—for example, a brief news summary might be ideal for the morning, as opposed to a long-form article, which might be better suited to the evening. This type of situational classification is important because it enables smart devices such as a speaker, connected car, or smart appliance to cater the information to a specific use case. This is one of the processes that help publishers make their content easier to discover and retrieve when a user is looking for a particular news item.

When publishers distribute content to a smart machine, the way that a device speaks relies on a language of categorization—a taxonomy. Words are organized into categories, such as whether they are referring to a person or a place or even a date, which then triggers an output. In voice-distributed journalism, this output (a story or other piece of news content) is then interpreted by a machine before it reaches its final audience.

3. **PRONUNCIATION GUIDES AND WRITING STYLE:** The new devices rely on text-to-speech technology to read the news. In some cases, these systems require extra help learning how to implement pronunciation hints and guidance for unusual names of people and places. This is particularly relevant when the news item includes names of foreign people or institutions.

What makes the pronunciation of certain names so difficult on these devices stems from the default language or dialect (for example, American English vs. British English) that a user selects when setting it up. Language and speech on voice devices are programmed through a finite process of phonetization and prosody that limits their ability to understand how a name should be pronounced if it doesn't fit into the parameters of the selected language.

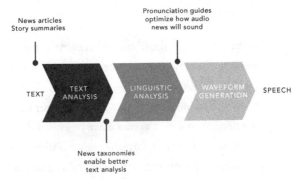

FIGURE 2.8: The process of converting text articles into audio alerts can be optimized through news taxonomies and pronunciation guides.

SPEECH TO TEXT: EXPEDITE
TRANSCRIPTION AND TRANSLATION

Speech-to-text systems can be used to help reporters and multimedia producers automate time-consuming, routine tasks such as transcription and captioning. Rather than sitting through hours of video or audio interviews and manually writing what the subject said, now reporters can use AI to get a text transcript automatically.

In the past, the Newsmaker had to upload the files she recorded on her smartphone to a computer and then play, fast-forward, pause, rewind, play again, and so on to find a certain quote; new applications allow the Newsmaker to highlight passages with a touch of a button, making routine postproduction tasks like transcript review, quote selection, and speech analysis much easier.

The BBC has developed one such tool, called ALTO, which uses text-to-speech technology to provide voice-over tracks for video content in multiple languages.[32] The software processes the video content into a transcript that is reviewed by an editor. The journalist then uses speech technology to automatically create a synthetic voice in a different language. Other media organizations, including ABC News, the *New York Times*, and ESPN, employ Trint, an AI software that uses technology similar to ALTO to turn interview audio files into text transcripts in real time.

When the Newsmaker attends a municipal community board meeting, this technology makes the reporting process much less labor-intensive. It's a three-hour meeting—normally a nightmare to transcribe. But the speech-to-text software quickly produces a transcript of the entire three hours, and the Newsmaker simply clicks and holds a button to highlight relevant segments of the meeting. Now, when the Newsmaker goes home, she doesn't have to listen to, much less transcribe, a three-hour recording.

GATHERING INFORMATION: SEEING WHAT THE NAKED EYE CAN'T

Computer vision and image recognition AI allow us to record what the eye can't see. In the newsroom, such tools can speed up the production and editing of photo and video. Meanwhile, entire stories might emerge as a result of recording data from visual cues that are too difficult to see or overwhelming to record.

The Newsmaker is using computer vision to track trains that have radioactive material by recognizing hazardous-material signage on train cars. If the national transportation board is claiming that no trains carrying hazardous materials pass through certain towns during school hours, a computer vision algorithm can detect if this is true by looking at the characteristics of trains that carry hazardous material and creating an automatic repository of this data over a few days, weeks, or months.

For another project, the Newsmaker was interested in mapping graffiti across her city, recording how patterns, colors, and occurrence vary across neighborhoods. By using computer vision to analyze several years of Google Maps Street View images, she was able not only to identify which areas of the city had the most graffiti, but also to examine changes resulting from gentrification, urbanization, or shifting industries; then she presented her findings in an online news interactive experience.

Image recognition also lets the Newsmaker automatically tag photos and videos in real time. For organizations like the Associated Press and Adobe with large photo archives, AI can generate granular metadata that improves image search. Another example is the *New York Times*'s partnership with Google to use computer vision to help digitize and organize its historical archive of 5 million photos.[33]

As with other types of AI, it's important for journalists to be attentive to how these systems are designed and the data used to train them. According to research conducted by MIT and Stanford University experts, an AI analysis of images of people with different skin tones and genders showed that the system was incorrectly labeling 34 percent of pictures of dark-skinned women, compared to just 0.8 percent for light-skinned men.[34] In response to findings such as these, IBM released a database with 1 million images for better analyzing human faces with diverse backgrounds.

These systems will inevitably reflect the bias in the training and prototypes used to develop them. Having the journalist making the final decision and regularly monitoring results helps ensure that any potential issues in the software are not transferred over into any published stories. Journalists should start the model evaluation process by asking: What can go wrong? In the particular case of classifying pictures of people, that means running different tests with images depicting individuals of different genders and with different skin tones, hair length, and other features such as glasses and piercings.

When deployed properly, AI has the potential to transform the way the newsroom operates. It enables journalists to work in smarter and faster ways, particularly when it comes to speeding up the postproduction process.

Typically, postproduction is the most time-consuming part of producing videos. It can take hours, if not days or weeks, to produce a video that's just a few minutes long.

Image recognition allows video editors to locate scenes and moments in raw footage—something that's traditionally been done through manual tagging, which is often inconsistent when done by multiple people. Finding specific shots in twelve hours of footage is no easy task. Even if editors are extremely organized and have tagged all the relevant shots, they still have to go through the entire twelve hours of video a few times to label them all. If journalists and editors can avoid the unnecessary process of searching, they can do more journalism.

At Comcast NBCUniversal LIFT Labs, AI specialists draw from the expertise of professional human editors to improve computer vision algorithms that can streamline video production. Similarly, CBS Interactive uses video recognition to automatically add metadata to their videos and improve content recommendations.

In her own newsroom, the Newsmaker applies a complex image recognition feature to search a sequence of shots from a local political rally for scenes in which counterprotesters appear. The image recognition software is able to make inferences about what identifies a "counterprotester," as opposed to someone attending the rally. Here, once again, machine learning and the proper training data become paramount, as they are what allow the software to recognize certain language on signs, how many people are reacting to

A CHECKLIST FOR
EVALUATING OVERALL
AI PERFORMANCE

- **ACCURACY:** Is the system consistently delivering reliable results? If errors occur, they should be documented and a plan for correcting it should be determined.

- **SPEED:** Once trained, does the AI perform its task quickly and without interruptions? The goal of leveraging smart algorithms is to expedite processes, but sometimes the software can be slow or difficult to use, and therefore reduce newsroom productivity gains.

- **SCALE:** Is the solution easily applicable to other parts or the newsroom? Newsrooms should avoid investing in AI that only solves a very specific, niche problem observed by a small group of people.

CONTINUED

- **INTEGRATION:** Can the tool be deployed to other existing newsroom systems? As more tools become available to journalists, the steps required to access them should be simplified. This includes integrating the solutions into the content management system or another centralized system used by the newsroom.

- **PRICE PERFORMANCE:** Are the costs of processing the data manageable? AI ingests enormous amounts of data, and that can be expensive. Journalists can partner with technologists to understand the best way to manage cloud computing costs.

an individual, or even certain facial features.

This is not all image recognition can do. In addition to creating complex tags for visual assets, image recognition can take those tags and link them with text stories. This is where automated text-to-visual platforms come in.

Automated text-to-visual platforms detect the topic of a text story and find correlated videos and images to add a multimedia element. A reporter might write an article, upload it to a platform, and a few seconds later have a fully relevant video piece to accompany the original article.

Software like this already exists, but growth in image recognition capabilities is making the output less noticeably templated, with improved graphics, better visual matching, and sophisticated video transitions. Today news organizations, including the French newspaper *Le Figaro*, the *Las Vegas Review-Journal*, and *USA Today,* use video automation tools to create content at scale and simplify their production workflow. Deploying this technology in the newsroom is helping the *Review-Journal* produce, on average, over four hundred videos each month, which represents a 372 percent increase in average monthly videos published compared to the previous year.[35] One of the positive results in terms of audience engagement is a 220 percent increase in its video views on Twitter. Online tools such as Wibbitz recognize visual elements in photos and videos and automatically match them with a text script that has been previously generated through natural language processing.

Although automated video is easy to create, journalists should be aware of the risk of overloading their audiences with too many visuals. Some stories may be better told in two paragraphs or even through a chart. Furthermore, an automated video created to go along with a more detailed report may be shared to a third-party platform without the report, and as a result not provide the full context to the viewer.

ROBOTICS: THE HARDWARE ENABLED BY AI

More sophisticated AI requires more sophisticated data inputs, which in turn require more sophisticated hardware for measurements. Cameras, infrared technology, drones, and sensors only scratch the surface in empowering journalists to gather data they would not be able to access otherwise.

Back in her newsroom's brainstorming meeting, the Newsmaker suggested using infrared cameras to spot audience excitement at political rallies during different points of a speech. Why? When humans get goose bumps, their temperature also increases. A rise in a group's collective temperature in under two seconds could potentially signify a strong emotional response to what the speaker has just said.

Using new equipment to measure things that a human can't comprehend is not as futuristic as it may seem. The Associated Press already uses hardware including motion capture suits, EEG sensors, and heart rate monitors to measure how news consumers engage with virtual reality journalism. All three technologies capture study participants' levels of attention and relaxation when consuming different types of content across devices. By working with data scientists, AP was able to derive editorial insights to help journalists understand how they should approach content creation. Data from the related 2017 study, *The Age of Dynamic Sto-*

rytelling, suggests that war zone reporting employing virtual reality technology drives study participants' "stimulation" and that the impact of the experience on them lasts longer than the impact of reading a comparable traditional story. On the other hand, science and environment stories build open-mindedness, associated with higher levels of relaxation.[36]

Beyond measuring audience engagement and informing content strategy, AI-powered robotics can aid with investigative work. In its 2016 Pulitzer Prize–winning investigation into abusive practices of the fishing industry in Southeast Asia, AP collaborated with commercial satellite company DigitalGlobe. The devices in orbit, which are powered by deep learning and object detection algorithms, was able to track boats carrying slaves.[37] This journalistic and technological endeavor resulted in the release of more than two thousand individuals who had been kept captive and forced into labor.

AI-powered hardware is also enabling new approaches to newsgathering. The *Capital Times*, a local newspaper in Madison, Wisconsin, leveraged an audio recording device developed by Cortico to collect conversations from small group meetings. The "digital hearth" allows journalists to better facilitate interviews by automatically playing excerpts from other groups to expose them to new ideas. The device is connected to an online platform that identifies recurring themes, helping reporters surface unique perspectives from local communities. Specific segments of the audio collected are then used within local journalism stories such as "Local Voices Network: Community Members Say More, Better

Public Transportation Needed."[38]

Elsewhere in the industry, robotics is automating the process of capturing photos and videos. The Walt Disney Company is improving its basketball and football TV coverage through machine-learning-powered cameras. These automated devices are learning from human operators how to track movements by players and generate smoother transitions in between scenes.[39] The goal of this effort, according to Disney, is to help humans be more aware of the sports they are capturing and reduce the number of cameras needed to cover any given game.

THE DARK SIDE OF AI: SYNTHETIC MEDIA AND THE NEXT GENERATION OF MISINFORMATION

In January 2019, a Seattle TV station aired video footage that appeared to show President Trump during an Oval Office speech sticking his tongue out at viewers. The video turned out to be doctored, created by splicing together real and fake footage with the help of artificial intelligence. The employee who released the footage was subsequently fired.[40]

Deepfake videos are one emerging pitfall of AI-driven content generation. They refer to images or audio files generated or altered with the help of AI to dupe an audience into thinking they are real. This recent example showed the dangers of a new technology that could be used for information warfare—and which has already been leveraged for nefarious purposes.

Deepfakes have risen in prominence in recent years as open-source code and tools have made the technology increasingly accessible. DeepFaceLab, for example, is an open-source code repository that allows users to easily swap faces of speakers in videos.[41]

The prospect of the next generation of misinformation is troublesome. For example, fake videos could make politicians appear to say controversial things or falsely implicate people in crimes. Image generation tools could be used to show people attending rallies they did not actually attend or to doctor archival images to support false narratives of history. False audio could make public figures appear to say things they don't believe in. Lawmakers including Sens. Mark Warner and Marco Rubio are already warning of scenarios like these.

The deepfake also poses a threat to journalistic trust and integrity. Now journalists must not only employ traditional fact-checking processes but also be vigilant about the possibility that video or image evidence could have been falsified. Publishing an unverified video that turns out to be fake or relying on falsified information as source material for a news story could stain a newsroom's reputation and lead to citizens losing faith in media institutions. Another danger for journalists is the potential for personal deepfake attacks—showing journalists in compromising situations or altering video footage of them—aimed to discredit and intimidate news outlets.

Because of these threats, it's important to understand this new form of media forgery. In response to the threat, the *Wall Street Journal* launched a forensics committee comprised of journalists from different departments who are being trained on how to use new tools to detect deepfakes.[42]

REPORTING ON AI AND ALGORITHMIC ACCOUNTABILITY

While using artificial intelligence for reporting presents one main avenue for such technologies, it will be equally important in the future for journalists to understand and report on AI itself and its impact. As AI shapes increasingly large swathes of daily life and society—implemented by businesses to determine product prices, governments to determine criminal risk, and doctors to customize medical treatment—readers will naturally turn to media outlets to make sense of the implications of these new technologies.

The Pew Research Center has found that Americans are concerned about the fairness and effectiveness of computer programs making important decisions in people's lives: at a broad level, 58 percent feel that computer programs will always reflect some level of human bias.

As mathematician and author Cathy O'Neil writes, "Algorithms are opinions embedded in code."[43] Increasingly, it is being acknowledged that AI software is prone to the same errors and biases that humans exhibit and can even exacerbate inequities, since AI is often implemented at massive scale, with little oversight. In an investigation by ProPublica into machine-generated criminal risk scores, reporters found the software to be biased against black defendants.[44] Reporting of this nature will be increasingly necessary for an algorithmically driven society to keep software accountable.

One challenge of algorithmic accountability reporting is bridging gaps in technical knowledge when writing about complex software for lay readers. Algorithms can be difficult

WHAT TO LOOK FOR WHEN ASSESSING WHETHER A VIDEO HAS BEEN FORGED WITH AI

- Flickering and blurriness around a subject's mouth or face

- Unnatural shadows or lighting, or irregular movements

- Discrepancies between a subject's face and body type

- Inconsistency between what's being said and lip movements

to explain to a large readership because they require technical knowledge, they are new and rapidly changing, and because private companies often keep the details of their operation under wraps. The complexity of algorithmic calculations can make it very hard to ascertain how an algorithm reaches a certain result. This is especially worrisome when we think about algorithms being used by the government to make decisions with wide-ranging consequences, such as in assessing the safety of air carriers or bridges.

Going forward, then, reporters must both deliver new insights using AIs and explain how they work and their impact. The difficulty of doing so is compounded by the fact that AIs are rarely built to explain their own decision-making. Northwestern University professor of computational journalism Nicholas Diakopoulos notes that these "algorithms sit in opaque black boxes, their inner workings, their inner 'thoughts' hidden behind layers of complexity."[45]

This is true in large part because AI systems are designed to perform certain functions, not to explain how they work.

In an article titled "Can AI be Taught to Explain Itself?," the *New York Times Magazine* described the limitations of the field of algorithmic explainability.[46] Probing these black boxes and keeping readers abreast of related developments are crucial goals of AI reporting.

When algorithms become widely used, when they fail, and when they are misused by humans, they can lead to significant consequences, such as discrimination, revenue loss, privacy breaches, and more. These are all instances worth investigating, because they impact everyday lives. The algorithms beat is relatively young, but it is likely to become more and more important as the adoption of algorithmic technologies by organizations and governments becomes widespread.

One example of algorithmic accountability reporting is the investigation by German Public Broadcasting into automated credit ratings.[47] Researchers looked at crowdsourced data from the secretive German credit rating agency Schufa as a way to provide some measure of oversight of automated rating systems, since governments and other rating agencies have not yet found a way to examine such methodologies.

ProPublica's journalistic series on machine bias and algorithmic injustice also pulled back the curtain on a number of automated processes. In one investigation, ProPublica partnered with the *New York Times* to find evidence that algorithms displaying online job ads discriminated against older workers.[48] The series also looked at racial discrepancies in auto insurance rates set by algorithms, which ended up costing those living in nonwhite-majority zip codes more.[49]

In another example, the *Wall Street Journal* showed how algorithms work by letting readers experiment with them interactively. The *Journal*'s article "What Can Algorithms Tell You About Your Writing?" invites users to enter text such as an essay or cover letter and receive results from an algorithm that rates the copy on the basis of tone, sentiment, and other semantic parameters.[50] In another story, *Journal* reporters explained, by annotating code, how a trading algorithm works.[51] These explorable explainers also include detailed methodology and source notes, which allow the *Journal*'s audience to understand the inner workings of a smart machine and how it is able to derive meaning from text analysis.

Exposing the inner workings of algorithms or uncovering their biases typically requires advanced computational journalism. It is often necessary to examine algorithmic processes through advanced technical tools:

- **SCRAPING DATA:** One pathway to understanding and analyzing algorithms, especially where their code is private, is to scrape public data. This means extracting large amounts of data from websites and saving it to a local computer in a structured format (e.g., a spreadsheet). Public data on rankings or pricing, for example, can help a journalist reverse-engineer an algorithm or at least spot notable patterns in its behavior. However, it should be noted as a potential pitfall that scraping might violate a website owner's terms of service agreement, and there may be other legal concerns, such as claims that scraping is a form of hacking in violation of the Computer Fraud and Abuse Act, as reported by *Fortune*.[52]

- **CROWDSOURCING DATA:** When it comes to personalized algorithms, it can be difficult to scrape data, since the algorithm's behavior will be customized to each individual user. In these cases, crowdsourcing data from the public may be necessary to learn more about the algorithm. ProPublica ran a program to crowdsource data on political ads on Facebook by having reader participants install a browser extension that automatically collected this data as they browsed their Facebook feeds. However, these methods can be contentious and may even be discouraged by tech companies. In ProPublica's case, their crowdsourcing effort was ended after Facebook limited its data access permissions for extensions like the one ProPublica was using.[53]

- **BOT PROGRAMS:** Bots can help assess how algorithms behave differently for various usage patterns, such as logging in from different locations, which could help someone evaluate geo-targeting. A bot is a program designed to conduct repetitive tasks on the internet; for example, visiting a website, clicking on a certain button or even uploading an image. Journalists can create bots able to perform these simple functions millions of times, allowing humans to understand how algorithms behave under different inputs. Though, again, as with scraping, there may be legal concerns with using bots, particularly around the use of any misleading or deceptive tactics.

It is imperative that newsmakers do not neglect transparency and explainability when applying AI to their own work. The practice of journalism is about questioning the world around us, and that same principle still applies even when a piece of software plays a role in a real-world decision. As artificial intelligence becomes more important, newsrooms will only become more crucial in holding algorithms accountable and explaining their behavior.

QUESTIONS THAT CAN HELP JOURNALISTS GUIDE THEIR RESEARCH INTO ALGORITHMS

- **CATEGORY:** What does the algorithm do (filtering, prediction, ranking, calculation, etc.)?

- **GOAL:** What is the algorithm optimizing for (e.g., maximizing time spent on site)?

- **DATA BASIS:** What data is the algorithm based on and is there any obvious bias in it?

- **TRANSPARENCY:** Is it clear and communicated to users how the algorithm makes decisions?

- **HUMAN OVERRIDE:** Is there oversight by humans able to quickly make decisions and tweak the algorithm?

- **EXPLAINABILITY:** Is the output of the algorithm explainable/interpretable?

- **DETECTED ERRORS:** Are there reported instances of mistakes the algorithm made?

- **FAIRNESS:** Are certain groups (dis)advantaged by this algorithm?

- **PRIVACY:** Is user data stored or shared with other users or third parties (e.g., advertisers, government)?

- **ROBUSTNESS:** Was the service checked for robustness against adversarial attacks and hacking?

3

WORKFLOW

A SCALABLE PROCESS FOR
NEWSROOM TRANSFORMATION

It dawns on the Newsmaker that the real impact of these artificial intelligence tools is the way they change how she works as a journalist. The challenge for media organizations is not only about access to technology but about finding the right model for integrating it into the newsroom.

Modern news companies need to do more than just understand AI. They need to become equipped to adapt to the disruptive changes that AI will bring to journalism, moving from a siloed workplace to a more responsive and collaborative one.

3.1. WHAT IS ITERATIVE JOURNALISM?

Traditional editorial strategies often lock out consumers from participation. By contrast, iterative journalism deploys new technologies to make the news process highly responsive to the needs of its readers or viewers. By understanding consumption data and by putting the storyteller's assumptions to the test, a newsroom can assess the value of a story *before* investing significant resources in it. This approach requires systematically integrating new technologies into traditional reporting processes at scale, rather than implementing new tools in one-off instances.

Iterative journalism is the idea of adjusting coverage in real time to serve the rapidly changing information needs of readers. This is possible by mixing editorial insights with audience feedback. Knowing which issues readers care about helps journalists to be accountable to them.

The iterative process starts with defining opportunities for news experimentation and identifying both the editorial resources needed and technical requirements. After launching a story prototype and measuring its audience impact, journalists evaluate whether the effort warrants additional commitment. If so, they can develop a scaling strategy, handing off the project to the proper group for the day-to-day management.

Implementing "minimally viable" stories, pursuing augmented audience understanding, and setting up research and development labs are three distinct strategies of iterative journalism that allow newsrooms to understand what variables of a story are most relevant to news consumers.

FIGURE 3.1: Iterative journalism is empathetic journalism. It uses audience interviews, surveys, experimentation, and observation to learn what readers care about.

"MINIMALLY VIABLE" STORIES

In 2018, Zurich-based media company Tamedia used text-generating bots to cover voting on various proposals across 2,222 Swiss municipalities. This type of reporting enabled the company to deliver updates customized according to a reader's location and thus to capture a so-called long-tail audience, where the largest portion of their readership had diverse editorial interests depending on what voting result was relevant to them.[1]

This new way of working emphasizes the importance of feedback as well as the need to focus on the different information needs of audiences. Tamedia was able to increase user engagement because their coverage was personalized by location.[2]

A "minimally viable" story is an article or news feature developed with sufficient information to satisfy initial information needs. A broader and more and comprehensive journalistic piece is only developed after considering feedback from the story's initial readers. Although this is an approach that can be effective for developing regular stories, it may not be applicable to some journalistic efforts, including investigations.

The Newsmaker regularly publishes automated stories and develops a sense of whether a particular topic is of interest to her audiences before investing too many resources into a broader journalistic effort. For instance, she used natural language generation and a dataset on recently released health indicators to produce hundreds of stories. From this, the Newsmaker notices that stories with information on childhood obesity appear to be important to her readers, based on high engagement metrics. The Newsmaker also implements the iterative approach by analyzing reader comments, to grasp how audiences engage with content published by her newspaper. Based on the data, she decides to further explore topics related to children's health.

She also urges her colleagues to move beyond the "publish and forget" mentality. The Newsmaker learns from her past work by documenting the successes and failures of her experiments with artificial intelligence.

Audience feedback can even happen in real time. The *Wall Street Journal* collaborated with Guardian Labs to seek immediate feedback from audience members who engaged with new types of stories and alerts on the U.S. Bureau of Labor Statistics jobs report.[3] Readers were invited to share their reaction to the *Journal*'s experiment by completing an online survey; the data collected from the survey was then used to improve the future strategy for live coverage as well as when to push out notifications.

These approaches have been difficult to apply in traditional journalism due to not only the limited opportunities for audience feedback but also the structure of work in the newsroom. Powered by new technologies and collaboration tools, iterative journalism can enable reporters to introduce their ideas to wider audiences without the risk of losing their scoop.

Still, applying iterative thinking to journalism is a balancing act. Technology usage and audience feedback can help journalists discover which stories connect most with news consumers without the risk of damaging journalistic integrity, voice, or message. At the end of the day, iterative journalism aims to empower news organizations to align their output with consumers' needs.

At the Newsmaker's company, this new approach is being tested with scheduled news events like election coverage and the Olympics. This gives her more time to listen to the audience, plan experiments, and bring colleagues into the process, without being tied to the daily news cycle.

RISKS FACING NEWSROOMS INTEGRATING THE ITERATIVE PROCESS

- Disruption of existing processes that are proven to work

- Pushback from colleagues who may be reluctant to change

- Lack of focus as a result of too much experimentation and testing

- A slower decision making process due to dependency on audience feedback

AUGMENTED AUDIENCE UNDERSTANDING

Iterative journalism begins with people but looks beyond demographic data to understand how individuals *feel* when they consume news. Knowing someone's age or gender, or where they live, might tell journalists something, but it doesn't tell them how to approach a story that is relevant for a certain community.

Traditional approaches to research and content development for online audiences lean on quantitative analysis. Newsrooms gauge the number of readers or viewers at different times during the day, access their basic demographic information, and see how they navigate the website. This might validate the Newsmaker's assumptions, but it doesn't actually tell her *why* her readers interact with stories and *what* they do with them. It's important to understand the behaviors and values of our audience. Iterative journalism is also empathetic journalism: it supplements data with audience interviews, surveys, and observation to learn what readers care about, not just how many of them there are. Many of these tasks can be done with the aid of AI.

At the *New York Times* and the *Washington Post*, artificial intelligence prioritizes certain reader comments for moderation by automatically flagging those with toxic or offensive language and by clustering contributions with similar viewpoints, enabling newsrooms to both expedite the evaluation of hundreds of thousands of comments and, at the same time, develop a deeper insight into how their audiences respond to certain stories or topics. This data can be used to inform future coverage.

Grasping audience values requires moving beyond engagement data points. The goal is to identify the issues that truly matter to a reader and the context in which news can be most useful for the audience. In this new landscape, reporters are not only interviewing their sources; they are also focusing on integrating their audiences and their colleagues into the journalistic process.

For example, business news channel CNBC runs a series called Ask Kensho, where viewers can tweet a business-related question and get an answer in near real time.[4] To accomplish that, the news station leveraged an AI-powered tool able to "find answers to more than 65 million question combinations by scanning over 90,000 customizable actions." These questions could also be used to understand what topics are relevant to viewers.

In Germany, *Die Zeit* polls its online readers on a daily basis to understand how they are reacting to current events such as an election result or even a protest. The dataset generated, a kind of "mood index," not only informs journalists about how readers feel but also forms the basis for new data-driven stories.[5]

By relying on both editorial expertise and reader feedback, newsrooms can put their audience at the center of the story development process.

This type of reader-centered approach in journalism is not without pitfalls. According to University of Oregon professor of emerging media Seth Lewis, inviting outside perspectives into the journalistic process can blur the lines between news professional and consumer, causing tension inside the newsroom.[6]

In fact, there is a danger of audience feedback having too much influence on what newsrooms decide to focus on. Stories of marginalized communities or complex subjects might not be of high interest to large numbers of readers but they are important issues to society as a whole.

To avoid the risk of losing sight of their own mission, newsmakers must create frameworks for audience participation that both take advantage of this new form of collaboration and maintain journalistic integrity.

RESEARCH AND DEVELOPMENT LABS

Implementing an iterative culture allows news organizations to quickly test new ideas and stay relevant. Many newsrooms are taking this principle to heart, setting up their own research and development functions to help journalists experiment with new approaches and disseminate best practices. Many of these new teams have been focused on artificial intelligence.

- BBC News Labs is set up as a multidisciplinary initiative implementing efforts such as semiautomated journalism and developing text-to-speech tools.[7] Some of its recent projects include an audiogram generator (a tool that turns audio files into videos for social media distribution) and chatbots that give audiences a conversational mechanism to learn about a certain story.

- WSJ R&D develops AI-powered tools and implements new processes such as verification of deepfakes and algorithmic transparency reporting. The team is also responsible for initiatives related to content automation using natural language generation and to text analysis tools using the latest developments in natural language processing.

- The *New York Times*'s research and development team focuses on areas including translation, computer vision, and sensors.[8] Beyond AI, the group explores other emerging technologies, such as blockchain, which can be used to fight misinformation by watermarking verified content and give audiences insight into the origins of news.[9]

- Quartz AI Studio is designed to help journalists use machine-learning methods to develop new types of stories.[10] One of those projects is Quackbot, among whose skills is that "given a topic, it can suggest some reliable sources of data."[11]

- The *Washington Post*'s R&D lab was launched in the summer of 2019 to experiment with computational journalism techniques to bolster coverage of the U.S. presidential campaign in 2020.[12]

Such groups are often established as a shared resource, accessible to anyone in a given newsroom. They serve as an interface for meeting challenges and helping colleagues identify opportunities through data-driven research.

The Newsmaker's editor recently created an internal fellowship program to give her colleagues the opportunity to spend two weeks working alongside technologists. Journalists are invited to submit proposals that are then reviewed by a cross-functional

COST-EFFICIENT WAYS TO
SET UP AN R&D LAB

- Tour academic research labs outside the news industry to learn best practices and bring in new ideas.

- Organize workshops where cross-functional teams are empowered to identify challenges and given time to experiment with new approaches.

- Establish an internal-rotation program where journalists get to spend a certain amount of time working alongside engineers.

- Host brown-bag lunches with external speakers from universities, start-ups, and other media organizations to discuss the latest research and deployment of new projects.

committee. Those who are accepted receive mentorship and get to develop projects related to areas such as AI.

3.2. ALIGNING JOURNALISM AND ARTIFICIAL INTELLIGENCE WORKFLOWS

The process of iterative journalism aligns closely with the attributes of artificial intelligence systems. Both begin with data collection. Then, AI expedites the process of observing and understanding context, which is also integral to the journalistic process.

Not only can AI help produce minimally viable stories for certain types of coverage, it can also assess the potential impact of a piece by gauging audience interest for a particular topic or theme. For example, while brainstorming stories about an election, the Newsmaker might turn to AI for surfacing insights about social media discussions. This can inform her about what topics are trending and what readers are interested in. By combining this information with her own journalistic instincts, the Newsmaker is able to find an angle that is both relevant and distinct. Data is everywhere but it's not everything. New data approaches, rooted in solid journalistic methods, strengthen the newsroom's understanding of the audience by providing the right context. This lets editors and reporters test the viability of a certain idea or news experiences before investing significant resources in pursuing it.

AI-powered tools such as NewsWhip have provided the *Guardian*, the *New York Post*, the Associated Press, the

Huffington Post, and other news organizations with a deeper understanding of their audiences and an ability to anticipate their needs. Mining social media and running sophisticated analysis of news coverage, this technology can monitor the public's curiosity about specific topics, then deliver that information to reporters via alerts and online dashboards.

The Newsmaker used a similar tool to identify a unique story angle after a politician announced a major tax break for multinational corporations. The machine learning system found that although there were hundreds of articles covering the politician's speech, there was significant social media chatter by individuals seeking clarification on the impact of this policy on small business owners. The Newsmaker used this insight to research the topic further and write an article addressing those unanswered questions.

In both iterative journalism and AI, learning from data and observation is fundamental in the development process. Through AI analysis of extensive data about people and their contexts, newsrooms can enhance audiences' experiences by understanding them better than ever before. In this way, both iterative journalism and machine learning incorporate human-centered design principles.[13]

3.3. THE THREE QUESTIONS OF ITERATIVE JOURNALISM

As newsrooms become more comfortable with experimentation, they should also consider the desirability of their stories or news products, the feasibility of having newsroom technology help create them, and the financial viability of a new journalistic approach.

DESIRABILITY

Does the news audience desire it?

VIABILITY

Is the news product or story methodology viable?

FEASIBILITY

Is the newsroom technically capable of doing it?

FIGURE 3.2: Iterative journalism borrows from design thinking methodologies, starting with the desirability of its audience, then answering questions related to feasibility of execution, and finally addressing its long-term viability.

QUESTION 1: DOES THE NEWS AUDIENCE DESIRE IT?

By better understanding the behaviors and interests of her readers and viewers, the Newsmaker is able to produce news relevant to them. Beyond testing audience interest through automated stories, it is helpful to invite news consumers to join reporters to discuss their changing information needs. These approaches can inject newsrooms with an audience-centric perspective.

To gauge audience interest in the topic of homelessness in the Bay Area, San Francisco public radio station KQED partnered with technology company Hearken to invite listeners to submit questions through an online tool.[14] Over a thousand submissions were centralized in a database and displayed for public voting. Journalists then focused on the most frequent questions—for example, "What are the most common causes of homelessness?"—to report on the issue. By listening to their audience KQED generated high audience engagement and produced stories that mattered to the community.

QUESTION 2: IS THE NEWSROOM TECHNICALLY CAPABLE OF DOING IT?

It's important for newsroom staff to understand the technical capabilities and limitations of technology. There are gaps in skill sets, of course, which can be addressed by hiring technical talent or through collaborations, but it's not enough to hire technologists and journalists separately. Moreover, many newsrooms will not have the financial resources to do so. Increasingly, a journalist will need to have technology skills, while technologists must understand journalism.

The rise of the journo-coder is chronicled in the book *Data Journalism: Inside the Global Future.*[15] Newsrooms are increasingly leveraging multitalented employees who understand both computer programming and investigative journalism. A case study of the *New York Times'* Interactive News Technology Department titled "The Journalist as Programmer," conducted by Cindy Royal, found that skills such as data analysis and statistics can augment traditional reporting techniques in an era where datasets are increasingly important to understand.[16]

But hiring technologists is not the only way to boost technical fluency. At the *Wall Street Journal*, editors sit alongside product managers. The goal: both teams collaborate and appreciate the other's perspectives. As a result, the *Journal* has been able to launch products that take into account insights from both teams.

QUESTION 3: IS THE NEWS PRODUCT OR STORY METHODOLOGY FINANCIALLY VIABLE?

Experimentation for experimentation's sake is a waste of resources, particularly for smaller newsrooms with financial and temporal pressures. The solutions developed in the context of iterative journalism must be financially viable. The Newsmaker understands that journalists today are more than storytellers—they need to understand how their organizations work and how their journalism is funded. But this doesn't mean that journalistic output should be determined by its financial viability.

By understanding how to build a sustainable model for news, newsmakers can more quickly launch and scale new ideas. This requires an open dialogue across editorial, product, and business teams. Journalism is increasingly shaped by individuals who build news start-ups or create digital-transformation projects within large media organizations.

A news organization can assess whether a news product is viable by evaluating risks, competitors, and success factors. The *Wall Street Journal*, for example, uses a specific methodology for evaluating projects, known as Objectives and Key

GUIDELINES FOR PAIRING JOURNALISTS AND TECHNOLOGISTS

- Meet regularly to explain how each side operates, as the workflows of journalists and technologists are completely different. For example, engineering teams operate with very clearly defined road maps, and any last-minute requests by the newsroom can have a big impact on the completion timeline. When working on a new product or tool, journalists should be comfortable with letting engineers complete their work before providing feedback.

- Develop a common language and avoid using specialized terms. An engineer might not be familiar with what "lede" or "kicker" means, and journalists might not know that AWS (Amazon Web Services) refers to a cloud computing platform. For the collaboration between teams to work, it's important to simplify the language as much as possible.

CONTINUED

- Define how each team will contribute to the project. It's important to delineate which decisions fall to the newsroom, which to the technical team, and which are a matter of joint responsibility. For example, an AI-powered content recommendation tool on the website requires technical considerations in terms of how it's built, but it also needs feedback from the newsroom to ensure the results are showing stories that are editorially relevant.

Results (OKRs).[17] This approach, which is also used by tech companies like Google, Intel, and Amazon, establishes measurable goals that align with the broader newsroom strategy for each team and individual.

The Newsmaker worked with her editor to establish the following OKRs for her team in this quarter. She focused on a small number of quantifiable results and made sure they represented a realistic challenge. She set them up quarterly.

OBJECTIVE:

- Increase engagement with local news content.

KEY RESULTS:

- Increase content production of local stories by 30 percent.

- Attract five thousand new subscribers by the end of the quarter.

- Pilot ten new story types across web and mobile platforms.

OKRs are an efficient way to evaluate the viability of new efforts and can be established at the individual, team, and newsroom level. This approach is enabling the Newsmaker to feel ownership of the strategic direction of the company, as if she were the CEO of a start-up. The idea of the "journalist as entrepreneur" is so important these days that journalism schools are emphasizing courses and training in product development and business planning. Among many examples, the CUNY Graduate School of Journalism offers a program in entrepreneurial journalism that teaches students new business models for news;[18] the Missouri School of Journalism runs an annual competition encouraging students to launch new start-ups that solve newsroom problems;[19] and Columbia Journalism School, recognizing the importance of understanding the business of news, has made a business course a mandatory part of its program.

3.4. PROMOTING COLLABORATION ACROSS THE NEWSROOM

The iterative process demands a new way of working and organizing inside the newsroom. Adapting quickly to new technologies and workflows requires the formation of multidisciplinary teams, made up of people with backgrounds in journalism, data science, design, technology, and strategy.

But what does it mean to create a context for collaboration? How can newsrooms create an environment for working together that does not feel coerced?

A first step is to reduce silos. The newsroom cannot be departmentalized if we expect rapid testing and cross-pollination between teams. This means the newsroom should be designed so that people with different backgrounds and skill sets regularly bump into each other. Such layouts facilitate the serendipitous collaboration that is more in line with the new dynamic model for news described in the first part of this book.[20]

Newsrooms are already starting to adopt this model. For example, the Associated Press's move to a new headquarters in downtown Manhattan in 2017 was marked by a drastic reduction in the number of individual offices and an increase in casual seating areas. The *Washington Post's* new office features numerous huddle spaces designed for informal gatherings and group discussions. At the same time, it's important to create spaces for people to be able to work alone when necessary. The *Wall Street Journal* installed phone booths throughout its offices so journalists could have privacy, and *Quartz* created café-style nooks ideal for private work sessions.

The point is that knowledge sharing involves more than explicit communication. It also calls for a culture where curiosity is not forced but surfaces organically, and an environment that encourages people to take risks such as implementing new AI technologies—which calls for collective trust, participation, and an expectation that the outcome may be imperfect.

Perhaps that is the most important thing to know about collaboration: it is messy and imperfect. But even if collaboration might sometimes seem counterproductive, because of clashes between personalities or a sense of bureaucratic delay, that doesn't mean it's not working. We tend to be focused on productivity, but the process of collaboration is often a sub-efficient process—we don't collaborate to achieve speed or ease of implementation; we do it to build something that includes multiple viewpoints.

THE STORY AS THE UNIT OF INNOVATION

Technology is always changing, but the constant in newsrooms is the storytelling and analysis. Building an iterative culture starts with a collective acknowledgment that it's okay to pilot, fail, and experiment.

Newsrooms that invest time in education become more flexible and continue to create storytelling that informs and delights their audiences. Building adaptability to new techniques depends on two core activities: training and research.

Newsroom managers can empower colleagues by providing them with new skills and a road map for creating change while eliminating internal constraints, for instance by allowing them to collaborate cross-functionally with other teams and, when possible, to work on the ideation of news products and tools. This empowerment includes exposing the newsroom to concepts like iterative journalism, but it could also involve teaching colleagues how to use new AI tools for data analysis or text and video generation.

Newsrooms will benefit from looking beyond their own walls for sources of inspiration. For instance, they might host an "innovator series" featuring speakers from outside the organization who can present fresh ideas related to media and journalism. But these training initiatives should not be top-down; the decisions about training should be sourced from journalists' needs.

Such efforts can have tangible impacts: the *Herald-Times* in Bloomington, Indiana, cites the five-hour-a-week training program it had in place between 2003 and 2006 as a factor in a 10 percent increase in newspaper sales and an improved online experience.[21] This initiative was successful because training activities were linked to very actionable goals.

Investing in training like this becomes paramount as AI rapidly changes the practice of journalism and affects how newsrooms are structured. In fact, training can reduce fears associated with the uncertainty of changing roles and inspire staff to become more enterprising in their work.

The professional organization Global Editors Network facilitates hackathons that bring together journalists from *National Geographic*, NBC News, the *New Yorker*, ProPublica, Vocativ, the *Washington Post*, and others to compete in the development of media industry innovations. Events like these offer an opportunity for reporters and editors to take a step back from the daily news cycle and think ambitiously about emerging forms of storytelling.

Working with universities and colleges can also enable newsrooms to develop new analysis and unique content. Take the *New York Times*'s collaboration with the Brown Institute at Columbia University, in an investigation of the emergence of bots across platforms like Twitter and Facebook. What initially started as a computational journalism classroom project led by Professor Mark Hansen later evolved into an immersive story that led federal authorities to investigate the sellers of fake followers.

CONCLUSION

Technologies like AI can augment—not automate—the industry.

In a journalism landscape altered by new technology, the next generation of newsmakers brings science to the art of storytelling. They are analytical about how they approach reporting and editing and focused on research and experimentation.

Newsrooms now have at their disposal the resources to scale production, free up journalists from time-consuming tasks, and simultaneously differentiate their reporting. Data and computer science are rapidly becoming integral to this process while changing how information is gathered, produced, distributed, and monetized.

Artificial intelligence tools can generate text directly from data, find hidden insights within video footage, transcribe and translate interviews in real time, and even create multiple versions of the same story. The adoption of AI in newsrooms also opens up new editorial roles, including automation editors, algorithmic accountability reporters, and computational journalists.

In this new editorial equation, technology is the variable and journalistic standards are the constant. AI is just another tool in the journalistic toolbox that can strengthen its depth and breadth, just as the revolutions of the internet, telephone, and typewriter once did.

AI may involve sophisticated algorithms, but the conclusions drawn by machines are not always correct. Journalists must always be questioning outcomes, validating methodologies, and ensuring explainability. This is no easy task: algorithms are difficult to audit and, as such, to hold accountable.

The insights generated through AI should be used as a compass that guides reporting, not as a clock that provides infallible information.[1] AI is created by humans, and it can make mistakes, often as a result of biases in how the AI was designed and in the data used to train it. The output is only as good as the input.

To put AI to good use, newsmakers across the industry must start experimenting with it. That doesn't mean journalists need to become technologists, but they do need to become more responsive to transformation. It's not about a particular technology; it's about editorial adaptability.

For newsrooms to succeed in this technological era, they need to deploy updated methods that can keep up with constant change. Iterative journalism begins with identifying the audience's information needs, through techniques such as minimally viable stories, augmented audience understanding, and accelerated research. Iterative journalism emphasizes feedback by cycling through several versions of an idea, bringing a product development mind-set to storytelling.

Combining journalistic intuition, powerful technology, and a culture of collaboration, iterative journalism enables news organizations to increasingly align their output with their consumers' demands.

The place where AIs can contribute to this process is in helping us understand news readers and contextualize what they care about. However, the proliferation of these smart algorithms has led some people to believe that the world can be quantified, reduced to numerical values, like when a machine extracts "sentiment scores" from a politician's speech or uses social media to measure public interest in a specific topic.

Journalists are attracted to this notion because the data extracted through AI may get them closer to the *truth*. Being able to use analytical signals can ground reporting in facts and even strengthen the notion that news can be a key source of guidance for society.

Yet if everything is boiled down to numbers, we lose sight of human nature. It becomes much more challenging to connect with news consumers when the coolness of data overtakes the warmth of storytelling.

Therefore, even though we have a surplus of data that can be mined and analyzed in mass quantities through AI, it is now more important than ever to put the human at the center of the process. Iterative journalism is not about "pivoting to AI"; it's about surrounding human reporters with AI that can augment their abilities.

The art of storytelling is the very fabric of journalism; it's what lets us connect and relate to others. AI will not replace journalism. Journalists will always need to put the pieces together, to construct narratives through which we understand the human experience.

The Newsmaker takes comfort in this, knowing that embracing AI has equipped her with a new set of tools to uncover the truth, while also knowing that no algorithm will ever take over her journalistic judgment.

ACKNOWLEDGMENTS

Many people supported me in the development of *Newsmakers*. Philip Leventhal, my outstanding editor at Columbia University Press, gave me the opportunity to explore the ideas in the book. Research assistants Kouroush Houshmand, Taylor Nakagawa, Lara Shabb, and Till Daldrup provided indispensable help. Kelsey Michael's crucial copyedits helped crystallize my ideas. Cynthia Hua conducted the technical review for the book.

Other helpful ideas, assistance, and inspiration came from the community at the Tow Center at Columbia Journalism School and colleagues at the Laboratory for Social Machines at MIT Media Lab. I thank my incredible colleagues at the *Wall Street Journal* and the Associated Press who have allowed me to be part of innovative newsrooms.

Finally, I wish to thank my parents, who have always instilled in me the importance of bridging art and science. My biggest thanks go to my wife and partner, Rachel, whose support has been crucial to the development of this book.

VISIT JOURNALISM.AI FOR ADDITIONAL RESOURCES.

NOTES

PREFACE

1.   PricewaterhouseCoopers, "Sizing the Prize: What's
       the Real Value of AI for your Business and How
       Can You Capitalise?," August 16, 2017, www.pwc.
       com/gx/en/issues/analytics/assets/pwc-ai-analysis-
       sizing-the-prize-report.pdf.

INTRODUCTION

1.   Max Willens, "Forbes Is Building More AI Tools
       for Its Reporters," Digiday, January 3, 2019,

digiday.com/media/forbes-built-a-robot-to-pre-write-articles-for-its-contributors/.

2. "AP to Preview Every NBA Game with Automation from HERO Sports, Data from Sportradar," *Sportradar*, January 24, 2019, sportradar.us/2019/01/ap-to-preview-every-nba-game-with-automation-from-hero-sports-data-from-sportradar/.

3. Shan Wang, "After Years of Testing, the Wall Street Journal Has Built a Paywall That Bends to the Individual Reader," Nieman Lab, February 22, 2018, www.niemanlab.org/2018/02/after-years-of-testing-the-wall-street-journal-has-built-a-paywall-that-bends-to-the-individual-reader/.

4. "World's First AI News Anchor Makes 'His' China Debut," Xinhua News Agency, November 8, 2018, www.xinhuanet.com/english/2018-11/08/c_137591813.htm.

5. U.S. Bureau of Labor Statistics, "Newspaper Publishers Lose Over Half Their Employment from January 2001 to September 2016," April 3, 2017, www.bls.gov/opub/ted/2017/newspaper-publishers-lose-over-half-their-employment-from-january-2001-to-september-2016.htm.

6. Aman Naimat, *The New Artificial Intelligence Market*, vol. 1 (Sebastopol, CA: O'Reilly Media, 2016).

7.   Diana Owen, *The State of Technology in Global
      Newsrooms* (2017 survey) (Washington, DC:
      International Center for Journalists, 2018),
      www.icfj.org/sites/default/files/2018-04/
      ICFJTechSurveyFINAL.pdf.

8.   David Levy and Damian Radcliffe, "Social Media
      Is Changing Our Digital News Habits—But to
      Varying Degrees in US and UK," *The Conversation*,
      December 19, 2018, theconversation.com/social-
      media-is-changing-our-digital-news-habits-but-to-
      varying-degrees-in-us-and-uk-60900.

9.   James L. McQuivey, with Carlton A. Doty
      and Ryan Trafton, *Will People Really Do That?*
      (Cambridge, MA: Forrester, 2015), www.forrester.
      com/report/Will+People+Really+Do+That/-/E-
      RES117907.

10.   "Social and Demographic Differences in News
      Habits and Attitudes," chap. 5 in *The Personal News
      Cycle: How Americans Choose to Get Their News*
      (Arlington, VA: American Press Institute, 2014),
      www.americanpressinstitute.org/publications/
      reports/survey-research/social-demographic-
      differences-news-habits-attitudes/.

11.   Nic Newman, et al., *Digital News Report 2018*
      (Oxford: Reuters Institute for the Study of
      Journalism, 2018), media.digitalnewsreport.org/
      wp-content/uploads/2018/06/digital-news-
      report-2018.pdf?x89475.

12.   "Xinhua Upgrades AI-Based News Production
        System," Xinhua News Agency, June 15,
        2018, www.xinhuanet.com/english/2018-
        06/15/c_137256200.htm.

13.   Katsuhiro Yoneshige, "About JX PRESS—
        English," JX Press, accessed June 19, 2019, jxpress.
        net/about/about-jx-press/.

14.   Shoko Oda, "This Media Startup Is Beating the
        Competition with a Newsroom Run by Robots,"
        Bloomberg, May 27, 2018, www.bloomberg.com/
        news/articles/2018-05-27/the-airline-geek-trying-
        to-build-a-media-giant-with-no-reporters.

15.   Chris Roush, "AP Biz Editor Gibbs to Oversee
        News Partnerships," *Talking Biz News*, July 21,
        2017, talkingbiznews.com/1/ap-biz-editor-gibbs-
        to-oversee-news-partnerships/.

16.   Zsolt Katona, Jonathan A. Knee, and Miklos
        Sarvary, "Agenda Chasing and Contests Among
        News Providers," Columbia Business School
        Research Paper no. 13-49, July 3, 2013, doi.
        org/10.2139/ssrn.2288672.

17.   Nicole Perrin, "Amazon Is Now the No. 3 Digital
        Ad Platform in the US," *eMarketer*, September 19,
        2018, www.emarketer.com/content/amazon-is-
        now-the-no-3-digital-ad-platform-in-the-us.

18.   Kevin K. Drew and Ryan J. Thomas, "From
        Separation to Collaboration," *Digital Journalism* 6,

no. 2 (2017): 196–215, doi:10.1080/21670811.20
17.1317217.

1. THE PROBLEM: A JOURNALISTIC MODEL IN TRANSITION

1.   Francesco Marconi and Alex Siegman, "A Day in
      the Life of a Journalist in 2027: Reporting Meets
      AI," *Columbia Journalism Review*, April 11, 2017,
      www.cjr.org/innovations/artificial-intelligence-
      journalism.php.

2.   Nic Newman, *Journalism, Media, and Technology
      Trends and Predictions 2019* (Oxford: Reuters
      Institute for the Study of Journalism, 2019),
      reutersinstitute.politics.ox.ac.uk/sites/default/
      files/2019-01/Newman_Predictions_2019_FINAL.
      pdf.

3.   Peter Aldhous, "We Trained a Computer to
      Search for Hidden Spy Planes. This Is What It
      Found," BuzzFeed News, August 7, 2017, www.
      buzzfeednews.com/article/peteraldhous/hidden-
      spy-planes#.mkqoYz91Q.

4.   "FT Introduces 'She Said He Said' Bot to Diversify
      Sources in Articles," *Financial Times*, November
      15, 2018, aboutus.ft.com/en-gb/announcements/
      ft-introduces-she-said-he-said-bot-to-diversify-
      sources-in-articles/.

5.   "JanetBot: Analysing Gender Diversity on the FT

Homepage," FT Labs, July 11, 2018, labs.ft.com/
product/2018/11/07/janetbot.html.

6. Will Mari, "Technology in the Newsroom:
    Adoption of the Telephone and the Radio Car
    from c. 1920 to 1960," *Journalism Studies* 19,
    no. 9 (2018): 1366–1389, doi:10.1080/146167
    0x.2016.1272432.

7. Reuters, "Reuters News Tracer: Filtering through
    the Noise of Social Media," Reuters Community,
    May 15, 2017, www.reuterscommunity.com/
    topics/newsroom-of-the-future/reuters-news-
    tracer-filtering-through-the-noise-of-social-media/.

8. "Conexiones entre políticos y medios en
    Twitter," *El País*, January 31, 2016, elpais.com/
    elpais/2016/01/29/media/1454086689_574154.
    html.

9. Dataminr, "Dataminr for News Enters Continental
    Europe, Signing Deal with France Info," September
    6, 2016, www.dataminr.com/press/dataminr-for-
    news-enters-continental-europe-signing-deal-with-
    france-info.

10. Antonis Kalogeropoulos, "The Rise of Messaging
    Apps for News," section 2.6 in *Digital News
    Report 2018*, by Nic Newman et al. (Oxford:
    Reuters Institute for the Study of Journalism,
    2018), media.digitalnewsreport.org/wp-content/
    uploads/2018/06/digital-news-report-2018.
    pdf?x89475.

11. Andrew Perrin, "Americans Are Changing Their Relationship with Facebook," Pew Research Center, September 5, 2018, www.pewresearch.org/fact-tank/2018/09/05/americans-are-changing-their-relationship-with-facebook/.

12. Media Cloud, "Media Cloud in Action: Case Studies," accessed June 19, 2019, mediacloud.org/case-studies/.

13. Alex Thompson, "Parallel Narratives: Clinton and Trump Supporters Really Don't Listen to Each Other on Twitter," Vice News, December 8, 2016, news.vice.com/en_us/article/d3xamx/journalists-and-trump-voters-live-in-separate-online-bubbles-mit-analysis-shows.

14. Sally Kestin, John Maines, and Dana Williams, "Speeding Cops Get Special Treatment, Sun Sentinel Investigation Finds," *South Florida Sun Sentinel*, February 13, 2012, www.sun-sentinel.com/local/fl-speeding-cops-culture-20120213-story.html.

15. *Radiolab*, "Cicada Tracker," WNYC Studios, accessed June 19, 2019, project.wnyc.org/cicadas/.

16. Stephanie Ho, "Sense It! A Beginner's Guide to Sensor Journalism," accessed June 19, 2019, www.stephanieho.work/sense-it/.

17. Tim Hwang, "Announcing the Winners of the AI and the News Open Challenge," Knight

Foundation, March 12, 2019, knightfoundation.
org/articles/announcing-the-winners-of-the-ai-
and-the-news-open-challenge.

18. Sahil Chinoy, "We Built an 'Unbelievable'
(but Legal) Facial Recognition Machine," *New
York Times*, April 16, 2019, www.nytimes.
com/interactive/2019/04/16/opinion/facial-
recognition-new-york-city.html.

19. Katerina Eva Matsa and Elisa Shearer, "News
Use Across Social Media Platforms 2018," Pew
Research Center, September 10, 2018, www.
journalism.org/2018/09/10/news-use-across-
social-media-platforms-2018/.

20. WashPostPR, "The Washington Post Launches
on Twitch," *WashPost PR Blog*, July 16, 2018,
www.washingtonpost.com/pr/wp/2018/07/16/
the-washington-post-launches-on-twitch/?utm_
term=.959a16de1e2b.

21. Sisi Wei, "Creating Games for Journalism,"
ProPublica, July 11, 2013, www.propublica.org/
nerds/creating-games-for-journalism.

22. Tristan Ferne, "Beyond 800 Words: New Digital
Story Formats for News," BBC News Labs,
September 26, 2017, medium.com/bbc-news-labs/
beyond-800-words-new-digital-story-formats-for-
news-ab9b2a2d0e0d.

23. Associated Press, "AP and Graphiq Expand

Collaboration to Offer Interactive Visualizations to all AP Customers," October 18, 2016, www.ap.org/press-releases/2016/ap-and-graphiq-expand-collaboration-to-offer-interactive-visualizations-to-all-ap-customers.

24. Michela Del Vicario et al., "Modeling Confirmation Bias and Polarization," *Scientific Reports* 7, no. 40391 (2017), doi:10.1038/srep40391.

25. Carl Benedikt Frey and Michael A. Osborne, "The Future of Employment: How Susceptible Are Jobs to Computerisation?," *Technological Forecasting and Social Change* 114 (January 2017): 254–280, doi:10.1016/j.techfore.2016.08.019.

26. Lucia Moses, "The Washington Post's Robot Reporter Has Published 850 Articles in the Past Year," Digiday, September 14, 2017, digiday.com/media/washington-posts-robot-reporter-published-500-articles-last-year/.

27. Zack Liscio, "What Networks Does BuzzFeed Actually Use?," Naytev Insights, accessed June 19, 2019, www.naytev.com/insights/what-networks-does-buzzfeed-use.

28. See, e.g., "Success Story: Hearst Television," True Anthem, accessed June 19, 2019, www.trueanthem.com/hearst-television/.

2. ENABLERS: THE AI TECHNOLOGIES
DRIVING JOURNALISTIC CHANGE

1. Roberto Brunelli, *Template Matching Techniques in Computer Vision: Theory and Practice* (Chichester, West Sussex: Wiley, 2009).

2. Jill Kirschenbaum, Adya Beasley, and Madeline Carson, "Voices from a Divided America," *Wall Street Journal*, October 29, 2018, www.wsj.com/articles/voices-from-a-divided-america-1540822594.

3. Sarah Slobin, "A Computer Watched the Debates. It Thought Clinton Was Happy and Trump Was Angry and Quite Sad," *Quartz*, October 21, 2016, qz.com/810092/a-computer-watched-the-debates-and-thought-clinton-happy-trump-angry-sad/.

4. Josh Chin and Liza Lin, "China's All-Seeing Surveillance State Is Reading Its Citizens' Faces," *Wall Street Journal*, June 26, 2017, www.wsj.com/articles/the-all-seeing-surveillance-state-feared-in-the-west-is-a-reality-in-china-1498493020.

5. Rigoberto Carvajal, "How Machine Learning Is Revolutionizing Journalism," ICIJ: International Consortium of Investigative Journalists, August 22, 2018, www.icij.org/blog/2018/08/how-machine-learning-is-revolutionizing-journalism/.

6. Jonathan Zittrain, "The Hidden Costs of Automated Thinking," *New Yorker*, July 23, 2019,

www.newyorker.com/tech/annals-of-technology/
the-hidden-costs-of-automated-thinking.

7. Alec Radford et al., "Better Language Models and
    Their Implications," *OpenAI Blog*, February 14,
    2019, blog.openai.com/better-language-models/.

8. Laurence Dierickx, "Why News Automation
    Fails," presented at the Computation + Journalism
    Symposium, Miami, FL, February 2019.

9. WashPost PR, "The Washington Post Experiments
    with Automated Storytelling to Help Power
    2016 Rio Olympics Coverage," *WashPost PR
    Blog*, August 5, 2016, www.washingtonpost.
    com/pr/wp/2016/08/05/the-washington-post-
    experiments-with-automated-storytelling-to-
    help-power-2016-rio-olympics-coverage/?utm_
    term=.85060ab27a8d.

10. Danny Robbins and Carrie Teegardin, "Still
    Forgiven: An AJC National Investigation," *Atlanta
    Journal-Constitution*, accessed August 26, 2018,
    doctors.ajc.com/.

11. Gabriel Dance and Tom Jackson, "Rock-Paper-
    Scissors: You vs. the Computer," *New York Times*,
    October 7, 2010, archive.nytimes.com/www.
    nytimes.com/interactive/science/rock-paper-
    scissors.html.

12. Mary Branscombe, "Artificial Intelligence's Next
    Big Step: Reinforcement Learning," *New Stack*,

January 25, 2017, thenewstack.io/reinforcement-learning-ready-real-world/.

13. John Glenday, "AI Artist Behind Art for Latest Bloomberg Cover," *The Drum*, May 18, 2018, www.thedrum.com/news/2018/05/18/ai-artist-behind-art-latest-bloomberg-cover.

14. Isabelle Didier and Philippe Raynaud, "Production automatique de textes: L'IA au service des journalistes," InaGlobal, February 9, 2018, www.inaglobal.fr/numerique/article/production-automatique-de-textes-l-ia-au-service-des-journalistes-10092.

15. E.g., "Résultats du second tour des élections départementales: Canton de Saint-Amour" (Results of the second round of elections: Saint-Amour canton), *Le Monde*, March 29, 2015.

16. *Los Angeles Times* (@LANow), "Please note: We just deleted an automated tweet saying there was a 6.8 earthquake in Isla Vista. That earthquake happened in 1925," Twitter, June 21, 2017, 7:01 p.m., twitter.com/LANow/status/877677781089304576.

17. Stuart Myles, "Photomation or Fauxtomation? Automation in the Newsroom and the Impact on Editorial Labour—A Case Study," presented at the Computation + Journalism Symposium, Miami, FL, February 2019.

18. Ralph Blackburn and Matthew Clemenson, "More Than a Quarter of Havering Children Obese by the End of Primary School, Says Public Health England," *Romford Recorder*, January 18, 2018, www.romfordrecorder.co.uk/news/health/more-than-a-quarter-of-havering-children-obese-by-the-end-of-primary-school-says-public-health-england-1-5359216.

19. "Craving Japanese? Check Out These 3 New Philadelphia Spots," Hoodline, January 24, 2018, hoodline.com/2018/01/craving-japanese-check-out-these-3-new-philadelphia-spots.

20. Tal Montal and Zvie Reich, "I, Robot. You, Journalist: Who Is the Author?," *Digital Journalism* 5, no. 7 (2017): 829–49, www.tandfonline.com/doi/

21. Mario Haim and Andreas Graefe, "Automated News: Better Than Expected?," *Digital Journalism* 5, no. 8 (2017): 1044–59, www.tandfonline.com/doi/abs/10.1080/21670811.2017.1345643.

22. Javier Zarracina, "The Words of Obama's State of the Union Speeches," *Vox*, January 14, 2016, www.vox.com/2016/1/14/10767748/state-of-union-2016-word-count.

23. Barbara Maseda, "Text-as-Data Journalism? Highlights from a Decade of SOTU Speech Coverage," *Online Journalism Blog*, February 5, 2018, onlinejournalismblog.com/2018/02/05/text-as-data-journalism-sotu-speeches/.

24. Inti Pacheco and Stephanie Stamm, "GE CEO Letters Decoded: Shrinking Ambitions and Disappearing Buzzwords," *Wall Street Journal*, March 1, 2019, www.wsj.com/articles/ge-ceo-letters-decoded-shrinking-ambitions-and-disappearing-buzzwords-11551441600.

25. Jeremy B. Merrill and Natasha Frost, "Here's What Lyft Talks About as Risk Factors That Other Companies Don't," *Quartz*, March 1, 2019, qz.com/1563668/lyfts-ipo-filing-highlights-risk-factors-other-companies-dont-mention/.

26. Sandra Peddie and Adam Playford, "Police Misconduct Hidden from Public by Secrecy Law, Weak Oversight," *Newsday*, December 18, 2013, www.newsday.com/long-island/police-misconduct-hidden-from-public-by-secrecy-law-weak-oversight-1.6630092.

27. "What Did Private Security Contractors Do in Iraq?," Overview, February 21, 2012, blog.overviewdocs.com/2012/02/21/iraq-security-contractors/.

28. Bloomberg Media Group, "Bloomberg Media's Innovation Lab Launches 'The Bulletin'—An AI-Powered News Feed for Bloomberg Mobile App Users," September 18, 2018, www.bloombergmedia.com/press/bloomberg-medias-innovation-lab-launches-bulletin/.

29. Youyou Zhou, "Analysis of 141 Hours of Cable News Reveals How Mass Killers Are Really Portrayed,"

Quartz, October 14, 2017, qz.com/1099083/analysis-of-141-hours-of-cable-news-reveals-how-mass-killers-are-really-portrayed/.

30. Nic Newman, *Journalism, Media, and Technology Trends and Predictions 2019* (Oxford: Reuters Institute for the Study of Journalism, 2019), reutersinstitute.politics.ox.ac.uk/sites/default/files/2019-01/Newman_Predictions_2019_FINAL.pdf.

31. Voicebot, *U.S. Smart Speaker Consumer Adoption Report 2019* (January 2019), voicebot.ai/smart-speaker-consumer-adoption-report-2019/.

32. "ALTO—a Multilingual Journalism Tool," BBC News Labs, accessed May 1, 2019, bbcnewslabs.co.uk/projects/alto/.

33. Sam Greenfield, "Picture What the Cloud Can Do: How the New York Times Is Using Google Cloud to Find Untold Stories in Millions of Archived Photos," *Google Cloud Blog*, November 9, 2018, cloud.google.com/blog/products/ai-machine-learning/how-the-new-york-times-is-using-google-cloud-to-find-untold-stories-in-millions-of-archived-photos.

34. Joy Buolamwini and Timnit Gebru, "Gender Shades: Intersectional Accuracy Disparities in Commercial Gender Classification," *Proceedings of Machine Learning Research* 81 (2018): 77–91, proceedings.mlr.press/v81/buolamwini18a.html.

35.   Wibbitz, "How Review-Journal Strengthens the Vegas
      Community Through Powerful Video Storytelling,"
      accessed June 19, 2019, www.wibbitz.com/resources/
      review-journal-local-news-video-case-study/.

36.   Francesco Marconi and Taylor Nakagawa, *The Age
      of Dynamic Storytelling: A Guide for Journalists
      in a World of Immersive 3-D Content* (New York:
      Associated Press, 2017), www.amic.media/media/
      files/file_352_1328.pdf.

37.   Robin McDowell, Martha Mendoza, and Margie
      Mason, "AP Tracks Slave Boats to Papua New
      Guinea," Associated Press, July 27, 2015, www.ap.org/
      explore/seafood-from-slaves/ap-tracks-slave-boats-to-
      papua-new-guinea.html.

38.   "Local Voices Network: Community Members Say
      More, Better Public Transportation Needed," *Capital
      Times*, March 25, 2019, madison.com/ct/news/local/
      local-voices-network-community-members-say-more-
      better-public-transportation/article_5aeeb82e-63e5-
      5a7a-a4b2-f50d01963706.html.

39.   Jianhui Chen et al., "Learning Online Smooth
      Predictors for Realtime Camera Planning Using
      Recurrent Decision Trees," IEEE Conference on
      Computer Vision and Pattern Recognition, Las
      Vegas, NV, June 27–30, 2016, hoangle.info/papers/
      cvpr2016_online_smooth_long.pdf.

40.   Kyle Swenson, "A Seattle TV Station Aired
      Doctored Footage of Trump's Oval Office Speech.

The Employee Has Been Fired," Washington Post, January 11, 2019, www.washingtonpost.com/ nation/2019/01/11/seattle-tv-station-aired-doctored-footage-trumps-oval-office-speech-employee-has-been-fired/?utm_term=.cdb970ea0968.

41. GitHub, "DeepFaceLab," accessed June 10, 2019, github.com/iperov/DeepFaceLab.

42. Francesco Marconi and Till Daldrup, "How the Wall Street Journal Is Preparing Its Journalists to Detect Deepfakes," Nieman Lab, November 15, 2018, www. niemanlab.org/2018/11/how-the-wall-street-journal-is-preparing-its-journalists-to-detect-deepfakes/.

43. Cathy O'Neil, *Weapons of Math Destruction: How Big Data Increases Inequality and Threatens Democracy* (New York: Crown, 2016).

44. Julia Angwin and Jeff Larson, "Bias in Criminal Risk Scores Is Mathematically Inevitable, Researchers Say," ProPublica, December 30, 2016, www. propublica.org/article/bias-in-criminal-risk-scores-is-mathematically-inevitable-researchers-say.

45. Nick Diakopoulos, "Algorithmic Accountability and Transparency," NickDiakopoulos.com, accessed June 10, 2019, www.nickdiakopoulos.com/projects/ algorithmic-accountability-reporting/.

46. Cliff Kuang, "Can A.I. Be Taught to Explain Itself?," *New York Times*, November 21, 2017, www.nytimes. com/2017/11/21/magazine/can-ai-be-taught-to-explain-itself.html.

47.   Uli Köppen, "Using Algorithms to Investigate
       Algorithms and Society," presented at the
       Computation + Journalism Symposium, Miami, FL,
       February 2019.

48.   Jennifer Valentino-DeVries, "AARP and Key Senators
       Urge Companies to End Age Bias in Recruiting
       on Facebook," ProPublica, January 8, 2018, www.
       propublica.org/article/aarp-and-key-senators-
       urge-companies-to-end-age-bias-in-recruiting-on-
       facebook.

49.   Jeff Larson et al., "How We Examined Racial
       Discrimination in Auto Insurance Prices," ProPublica,
       April 5, 2017, www.propublica.org/article/minority-
       neighborhoods-higher-car-insurance-premiums-
       methodology.

50.   Nigel Chiwaya, "What Can Algorithms Tell You
       About Your Writing?," *Wall Street Journal*, May 21,
       2018, www.wsj.com/graphics/what-algorithms-can-
       tell-you-about-your-writing/.

51.   Bradley Hope, "Decoded: Breaking Down How an
       Actual Trading Algorithm Works," May 22, 2017,
       Wall Street Journal, www.wsj.com/graphics/journey-
       inside-a-real-life-trading-algorithm/.

52.   Jeff John Roberts, "News Sites That Take on Big
       Tech Face Legal Peril," *Fortune*, September 27, 2018,
       fortune.com/2018/09/27/facebook-research-
       censorship/.

53.   Jeremy B. Merrill et al., "Facebook Political Ad
       Collector: How Political Advertisers Target You,"

ProPublica, July 17, 2018, projects.propublica.org/
facebook-ads/.

3. WORKFLOW: A SCALABLE PROCESS FOR
NEWSROOM TRANSFORMATION

1. Titus Plattner and Didier Orel, "Addressing Micro-
    Audiences at Scale," presented at the Computation
    + Journalism Symposium, Miami, FL, February
    2019.

2. Heather Chaplin, "Guide to Journalism and
    Design," *Columbia Journalism Review*, July 13,
    2016, www.cjr.org/tow_center_reports/guide_to_
    journalism_and_design.php/.

3. Shan Wang, "The Wall Street Journal Tested Live
    Push Notifications, with Some Help from the
    Guardian's Mobile Lab," Nieman Lab, August 4,
    2017, www.niemanlab.org/2017/08/the-wall-
    street-journal-tested-live-push-notifications-with-
    some-help-from-the-guardians-mobile-lab/.

4. Kristin Cwalinski, "What Is Kensho?," CNBC,
    April 15, 2015, www.cnbc.com/2015/04/15/sho.
    html.

5. Julian Stahnke et al. "Stimmungskurven: Wie
    geht es uns?" (Mood curves: How are we
    doing?), *Die Zeit*, March 23, 2017, www.zeit.de/
    gesellschaft/2017-03/stimmung-wie-geht-es-uns.

6. Seth C. Lewis, "The Tension Between Professional
    Control and Open Participation," *Information,*

Communication, and Society 15, no. 6 (2011): 836–866, doi:10.1080/1369118x.2012.674150.

7. "Stories by Numbers: Experimenting with Semi-Automated Journalism," BBC News Labs, March 22, 2019, bbcnewslabs.co.uk/2019/03/22/stories-by-numbers/.

8. Kinsey Wilson, "Note from Kinsey Wilson: Marc Lavallee to Head Story[X]," New York Times Company, September 7, 2016, www.nytco.com/press/note-from-kinsey-wilson-marc-lavallee-to-head-storyx/.

9. Sasha Koren, "Introducing the News Provenance Project," Times Open, July 23, 2019, open.nytimes.com/introducing-the-news-provenance-project-723dbaf07c44.

10. John Keefe, "Announcing the Quartz AI Studio, Designed to Help Journalists Use Machine Learning," *Quartz*, November 20, 2018, qz.com/1464390/announcing-the-quartz-ai-studio-designed-to-help-journalists-use-machine-learning/.

11. John Keefe, "Announcing Quackbot, a Slack Bot for Journalists from Quartz and DocumentCloud," Quartz Bot Studio, October 3, 2017, bots.qz.com/1455/announcing-quackbot-a-slack-bot-for-journalists-from-quartz-and-documentcloud/.

12. "The Washington Post Establishes a Computational Political Journalism R&D Lab to Augment Its Campaign 2020 Coverage," *WashPost*

PR Blog, July 24, 2019, www.washingtonpost.com/
pr/2019/07/24/washington-post-establishes-
computational-political-journalism-rd-lab-
augment-its-campaign-coverage/.

13. John Morley, "A Blueprint for Better Program
Design," LinkedIn, March 27, 2017, www.linkedin.
com/pulse/blueprint-better-program-design-john-
morley/.

14. Julia Haslanger, "Hearken Case Study: KQED
Gathered 1,300+ Questions About Homelessness,"
Hearken, November 6, 2016, medium.com/we-are-
hearken/hearken-case-study-kqed-gathered-1–300-
questions-about-homelessness-4939d63a2a46.

15. Tom Felle, John Mair, and Damian Radcliffe, eds.,
Data Journalism: Inside the Global Future (Bury St.
Edmunds, Suffolk, UK: Abramis, 2015).

16. Cindy Royal, "The Journalist as Programmer: A
Case Study of *The New York Times* Interactive
News Technology Department," *International
Symposium on Online Journalism* 2, no. 1 (2012),
www.isoj.org/wp-content/uploads/2016/10/
ISOJ_Journal_V2_N1_2012_Spring.pdf.

17. Kathryn Thomas, "How the WSJ iOS Team
Promotes Cross-Team Collaboration Through
OKR-Driven Feature Requests," *Dow Jones Tech*,
May 29, 2018, medium.com/dowjones/how-the-
wsj-ios-team-promotes-cross-team-collaboration-
through-okr-driven-feature-requests-a3f534bcccb.

18. Newmark J-School Staff, "Entrepreneurial

Journalism Initiative Kicks Off with Five New
Courses," CUNY Newmark Graduate School of
Journalism, February 14, 2011, www.journalism.
cuny.edu/2011/02/entrepreneurial-journalism-
certificate-program-opens-for-business/.

19.   "Missouri Business Alert: 4 MU Startups Secure
First Investments from $2.1M Accelerator Fund,"
Donald W. Reynolds Journalism Institute,
November 16, 2016, www.rjionline.org/stories/
missouri-business-alert-4-mu-startups-secure-first-
investments-from-2.1m-ac.

20.   Dana Coester, *A Matter of Space: Designing
Newsrooms for New Digital Practice* (Arlington,
VA: American Press Institute, 2017), www.
americanpressinstitute.org/publications/reports/
strategy-studies/matter-of-space/.

21.   Michele McLellan and Tim Porter, *News,
Improved: How America's Newsrooms Are Learning
to Change* (Washington, DC: CQ Press, 2007).

CONCLUSION

1.   Michele Mezza, *Algoritmi di libertà: La potenza
del calcolo tra dominio e conflitto* (Algorithms
of freedom: Computational power between
domination and conflict) (Rome: Donzelli Editore,
2018).

BIBLIOGRAPHY

Aldhous, Peter. "We Trained a Computer to Search for Hidden Spy Planes. This Is What It Found." BuzzFeed News, August 7, 2017. www. buzzfeednews.com/article/peteraldhous/hidden-spy-planes#. mkqoYz91Q.

American Press Institute. "Social and Demographic Differences in News Habits and Attitudes." Chap. 5 in *The Personal News Cycle: How American Choose to Get Their News*. Arlington, VA: American Press Institute, 2014. www.americanpressinstitute. org/publications/reports/survey-research/social-demographic- differences-news-habits-attitudes/.

Angwin, Julia, and Jeff Larson. "Bias in Criminal Risk Scores Is Mathematically Inevitable, Researchers Say." ProPublica, December 30, 2016. www.propublica.org/article/bias-in- criminal-risk-scores-is-mathematically-inevitable-researchers-say.

BIBLIOGRAPHY

BBC News Labs. "ALTO—a Multilingual Journalism Tool." Accessed May
    1, 2019. bbcnewslabs.co.uk/projects/alto/.

BBC News Labs. "Stories by Numbers: Experimenting with Semi-
    Automated Journalism." March 22, 2019. bbcnewslabs.
    co.uk/2019/03/22/stories-by-numbers/.

Blackburn, Ralph, and Matthew Clemenson. "More Than a Quarter of
    Havering Children Obese by the End of Primary School, Says
    Public Health England." *Romford Recorder*, January 18, 2018.
    www.romfordrecorder.co.uk/news/health/more-than-a-quarter-
    of-havering-children-obese-by-the-end-of-primary-school-says-
    public-health-england-1-5359216.

Bloomberg Media Group. "Bloomberg Media's Innovation Lab Launches
    'The Bulletin'—An AI-Powered News Feed for Bloomberg
    Mobile App Users." September 18, 2018. www.bloombergmedia.
    com/press/bloomberg-medias-innovation-lab-launches-bulletin/.

Branscombe, Mary. "Artificial Intelligence's Next Big Step: Reinforcement
    Learning." *New Stack*, January 26, 2017. thenewstack.io/
    reinforcement-learning-ready-real-world/.

Brunelli, Roberto. *Template Matching Techniques in Computer Vision:
    Theory and Practice*. Chichester, West Sussex: Wiley, 2009.

Buolamwini, Joy, and Timnit Gebru. "Gender Shades: Intersectional
    Accuracy Disparities in Commercial Gender Classification."
    Proceedings of Machine Learning Research 81 (2018): 77–91.
    proceedings.mlr.press/v81/buolamwini18a.html.

Capital Times. "Local Voices Network: Community Members Say More,
    Better Public Transportation Needed." March 25, 2019. madison.
    com/ct/news/local/local-voices-network-community-members-

say-more-better-public-transportation/article_5aeeb82e-63e5-
5a7a-a4b2-f50d01963706.html.

Carvajal, Rigoberto. "How Machine Learning Is Revolutionizing
Journalism." ICIJ: International Consortium of Investigative
Journalism, August 22, 2018. www.icij.org/blog/2018/08/how-
machine-learning-is-revolutionizing-journalism/.

Chaplin, Heather. "Guide to Journalism and Design." *Columbia Journalism
Review*, July 13, 2016. www.cjr.org/tow_center_reports/guide_
to_journalism_and_design.php/.

Chen, Jianhui, Hoang M. Le, Peter Carr, Yisong Yue, and James J. Little.
"Learning Online Smooth Predictors for Realtime Camera
Planning Using Recurrent Decision Trees." IEEE Conference on
Computer Vision and Pattern Recognition, Las Vegas, NV, June
27–30, 2016. hoangle.info/papers/cvpr2016_online_smooth_
long.pdf.

Chin, Josh, and Liza Lin. "China's All-Seeing Surveillance State Is Reading
Its Citizens' Faces." *Straits Times* (Singapore), July 7, 2017. www.
straitstimes.com/opinion/chinas-all-seeing-surveillance-state-is-
reading-its-citizens-faces.

Chinoy, Sahil. "We Built an 'Unbelievable' (but Legal) Facial Recognition
Machine." *New York Times*, April 16, 2019. www.nytimes.com/
interactive/2019/04/16/opinion/facial-recognition-new-york-
city.html.

Chiwaya, Nigel. "What Can Algorithms Tell You About Your Writing?"
Wall Street Journal, May 21, 2018. www.wsj.com/graphics/what-
algorithms-can-tell-you-about-your-writing/.

Coester, Dana. *A Matter of Space: Designing Newsrooms for New Digital*

Practice. Arlington, VA: American Press Institute, 2017. www.americanpressinstitute.org/publications/reports/strategy-studies/matter-of-space/.

Confessore, Nicholas, Gabriel J. X. Dance, Richard Harris, and Mark Hansen. "The Follower Factory." *New York Times*, January 27, 2018. www.nytimes.com/interactive/2018/01/27/technology/social-media-bots.html.

Confessore, Nicholas, Gabriel J. X. Dance, and Rich Harris. "Twitter Followers Vanish Amid Inquiries into Fake Accounts." *New York Times*, January 31, 2018. www.nytimes.com/interactive/2018/01/31/technology/social-media-bots-investigations.html.

Cwalinski, Kristin. "What Is Kensho?" CNBC, April 15, 2015. www.cnbc.com/2015/04/15/sho.html.

Dance, Gabriel, and Tom Jackson. "Rock-Paper-Scissors: You vs. the Computer." *New York Times*, October 7, 2010. archive.nytimes.com/www.nytimes.com/interactive/science/rock-paper-scissors.html.

Dataminr. "Dataminr for News Enters Continental Europe, Signing Deal with France Info." September 6, 2016. www.dataminr.com/press/dataminr-for-news-enters-continental-europe-signing-deal-with-france-info.

Del Vicario, Michela, Antonio Scala, Guido Caldarelli, H. Eugene Stanley, and Walter Quattrociocchi. "Modeling Confirmation Bias and Polarization." *Scientific Reports* 7, no. 40391 (2017). doi:10.1038/srep40391.

Diakopoulos, Nick. "Algorithmic Accountability and Transparency."

NickDiakopoulos.com, accessed June 10, 2019. www. nickdiakopoulos.com/projects/algorithmic-accountability-reporting/.

Didier, Isabelle, and Philippe Raynaud. "Production automatique de textes: L'IA au service des journalistes." InaGlobal, November 19, 2013. www.inaglobal.fr/numerique/article/production-automatique-de-textes-l-ia-au-service-des-journalistes-10092.

Dierickx, Laurence. "Why News Automation Fails." Presented at the Computation + Journalism Symposium, Miami, FL, February 2019.

Donald W. Reynolds Journalism Institute. "Missouri Business Alert: 4 MU Startups Secure First Investments from $2.1M Accelerator Fund." November 16, 2016. www.rjionline.org/stories/missouri-business-alert-4-mu-startups-secure-first-investments-from-2.1m-ac.

Drew, Kevin K., and Ryan J. Thomas. "From Separation to Collaboration." *Digital Journalism* 6, no. 2 (2017): 196–215. doi:10.1080/21670 811.2017.1317217.

El País. "Conexiones entre políticos y medios en Twitter." January 31, 2016. elpais.com/elpais/2016/01/29/media/1454086689_574154. html.

Felle, Tom, John Mair, and Damian Radcliffe, eds. *Data Journalism: Inside the Global Future*. Bury St. Edmunds, Suffolk, UK: Abramis, 2015.

Ferne, Tristan. "Beyond 800 Words: New Digital Story Formats for News." BBC News Labs, September 26, 2017. medium.com/bbc-news-labs/beyond-800-words-new-digital-story-formats-for-news-ab9b2a2d0e0d.

Financial Times. "FT Introduces 'She Said He Said' Bot to Diversify
	Sources in Articles." November 15, 2018. aboutus.ft.com/en-gb/
	announcements/ft-introduces-she-said-he-said-bot-to-diversify-
	sources-in-articles/.

Frey, Carl Benedikt, and Michael A. Osborne. "The Future of Employment:
	How Susceptible Are Jobs to Computerisation?" *Technological
	Forecasting and Social Change* 114 (2017): 254–80.
	doi:10.1016/j.techfore.2016.08.019.

FT Labs. "JanetBot: Analysing Gender Diversity on the FT Homepage."
	July 11, 2018. labs.ft.com/product/2018/11/07/janetbot.html.

GitHub. "DeepFaceLab." Accessed June 10, 2019. github.com/iperov/
	DeepFaceLab.

Glenday, John. "AI Artist Behind Art for Latest Bloomberg Cover." *The
	Drum*, May 18, 2018. www.thedrum.com/news/2018/05/18/ai-
	artist-behind-art-latest-bloomberg-cover.

Greenfield, Sam. "Picture What the Cloud Can Do: How the New York
	Times Is Using Google Cloud to Find Untold Stories in Millions
	of Archived Photos." *Google Cloud Blog*, November 9, 2018.
	cloud.google.com/blog/products/ai-machine-learning/how-the-
	new-york-times-is-using-google-cloud-to-find-untold-stories-in-
	millions-of-archived-photos.

Haim, Mario, and Andreas Graefe. "Automated News: Better Than
	Expected?" *Digital Journalism* 5, no. 8 (2017): 1044–59. www.
	tandfonline.com/doi/abs/10.1080/21670811.2017.1345643.

Haslanger, Julia. "Hearken Case Study: KQED Gathered 1,300+ Questions
	About Homelessness." Hearken, November 16, 2016. medium.
	com/we-are-hearken/hearken-case-study-kqed-gathered-1–300-

questions-about-homelessness-4939d63a2a46.

Ho, Stephanie. "Sense It! A Beginner's Guide to Sensor Journalism." Accessed June 19, 2019. www.stephanieho.work/sense-it/.

Hoodline. "Craving Japanese? Check Out These 3 New Philadelphia Spots." January 24, 2018. hoodline.com/2018/01/craving-japanese-check-out-these-3-new-philadelphia-spots.

Hope, Bradley. "Decoded: Breaking Down How an Actual Trading Algorithm Works." *Wall Street Journal*, May 22, 2017. www.wsj.com/graphics/journey-inside-a-real-life-trading-algorithm/.

Hwang, Tim. "Announcing the Winners of the AI and the News Open Challenge." Knight Foundation, March 12, 2019. knightfoundation.org/articles/announcing-the-winners-of-the-ai-and-the-news-open-challenge.

Kalogeropoulos, Antonis. "The Rise of Messaging Apps for News." Section 2.6 in Nic Newman et al., *Digital News Report 2018*. www.digitalnewsreport.org/survey/2018/the-rise-of-messaging-apps-for-news/.

Katona, Zsolt, Jonathan A. Knee, and Miklos Sarvary. "Agenda Chasing and Contests Among News Providers." Columbia Business School Research Paper no. 13-49, July 3, 2013. doi:10.2139/ssrn.2288672.

Keefe, John. "Annoucing Quackbot, a Slack Bot for Journalists from Quartz and DocumentCloud." Quartz Bot Studio, October 3, 2017. bots.qz.com/1455/announcing-quackbot-a-slack-bot-for-journalists-from-quartz-and-documentcloud/.

Keefe, John. "Announcing the Quartz AI Studio, Designed to Help Journalists Use Machine Learning." *Quartz*, November 20, 2018.

qz.com/1464390/announcing-the-quartz-ai-studio-designed-to-help-journalists-use-machine-learning/.

Kestin, Sally, John Maines, and Dana Williams. "Speeding Cops Get Special Treatment, Sun Sentinel Investigation Finds." *South Florida Sun Sentinel*, February 13, 2012. www.sun-sentinel.com/local/fl-speeding-cops-culture-20120213-story.html.

Kirschenbaum, Jill, Adya Beasley, and Madeline Carson. "Voices from a Divided America." *Wall Street Journal*, October 29, 2018. www.wsj.com/articles/voices-from-a-divided-america-1540822594.

Köppen, Uli. "Using Algorithms to Investigate Algorithms and Society." Presented at the Computation + Journalism Symposium, Miami, FL, February 2019.

Koren, Sasha. "Introducing the News Provenance Project." Times Open, July 23, 2019, open.nytimes.com/introducing-the-news-provenance-project-723dbaf07c44.

Kuang, Cliff. "Can A.I. Be Taught to Explain Itself?" *New York Times*, November 21, 2017. www.nytimes.com/2017/11/21/magazine/can-ai-be-taught-to-explain-itself.html.

Larson, Jeff, Julia Angwin, Lauren Kirchner, and Surya Mattu. "How We Examined Racial Discrimination in Auto Insurance Prices." ProPublica, April 5, 2017. www.propublica.org/article/minority-neighborhoods-higher-car-insurance-premiums-methodology.

Levy, David, and Damian Radcliffe. "Social Media Is Changing Our Digital News Habits—but to Varying Degrees in US and UK." *The Conversation*, December 19, 2018. theconversation.com/social-media-is-changing-our-digital-news-habits-but-to-varying-degrees-in-us-and-uk-60900.

Lewis, Seth C. "The Tension Between Professional Control and Open
    Participation." *Information, Communication, and Society* 15, no. 6
    (2011): 836–866. doi:10.1080/1369118x.2012.674150.

Liscio, Zack. "What Networks Does BuzzFeed Actually Use?" Naytev
    Insights, accessed June 19, 2019. www.naytev.com/insights/what-
    networks-does-buzzfeed-use.

Los Angeles Times (@LANow). "Please note: We just deleted an automated
    tweet saying there was a 6.8 earthquake in Isla Vista. That
    earthquake happened in 1925." Twitter, June 21, 2017, 7:01 p.m.
    twitter.com/LANow/status/877677781089304576.

Marconi, Francesco, and Till Daldrup. "How the Wall Street Journal Is
    Preparing Its Journalists to Detect Deepfakes." Nieman Lab,
    November 15, 2018. www.niemanlab.org/2018/11/how-
    the-wall-street-journal-is-preparing-its-journalists-to-detect-
    deepfakes/.

Marconi, Francesco, and Taylor Nakagawa. *The Age of Dynamic Storytelling:
    A Guide for Journalists in a World of Immersive 3-D Content.* New
    York: Associated Press, 2017. www.amic.media/media/files/
    file_352_1328.pdf.

Marconi, Francesco, and Alex Siegman. "A Day in the Life of a Journalist
    in 2027: Reporting Meets AI." *Columbia Journalism Review,*
    April 11, 2017. www.cjr.org/innovations/artificial-intelligence-
    journalism.php.

Marconi, Francesco, and Alex Siegman. *The Future of Augmented
    Journalism: A Guide for Newsrooms in the Age of Smart Machines.*
    New York: Associated Press, 2017.

Mari, Will. "Technology in the Newsroom." *Journalism Studies* 19, no. 9

(2018): 1366–1389. doi:10.1080/1461670x.2016.1272432.

Maseda, Barbara. "Text-as-Data Journalism? Highlights from a Decade of SOTU Speech Coverage." *Online Journalism Blog*, February 5, 2018. onlinejournalismblog.com/2018/02/05/text-as-data-journalism-sotu-speeches/#more-25542.

Matsa, Katerina Eva, and Elisa Shearer. "News Use Across Social Media Platforms 2018." Pew Research Center, September 10, 2018. www.journalism.org/2018/09/10/news-use-across-social-media-platforms-2018/.

McDowell, Robin, Martha Mendoza, and Margie Mason. "AP Tracks Slave Boats to Papua New Guinea." Associated Press, July 27, 2015. www.ap.org/explore/seafood-from-slaves/ap-tracks-slave-boats-to-papua-new-guinea.html.

McLellan, Michele, and Tim Porter. *News, Improved: How America's Newsrooms Are Learning to Change*. Washington, DC: CQ Press, 2007.

McQuivey, James L., with Carlton A. Doty and Ryan Trafton. *Will People Really Do That?* Cambridge, MA: Forrester, 2015. www.forrester.com/report/Will+People+Really+Do+That/-/E-RES117907.

Media Cloud. "Media Cloud in Action: Case Studies." Accessed June 19, 2019. mediacloud.org/case-studies/.

Merrill, Jeremy B., and Natasha Frost. "Here's What Lyft Talks About as Risk Factors That Other Companies Don't." *Quartz*, March 1, 2019. qz.com/1563668/lyfts-ipo-filing-highlights-risk-factors-other-companies-dont-mention/.

Merrill, Jeremy B., Ally J. Levine, Ariana Tobin, Jeff Larson, and Julia Angwin. "Facebook Political Ad Collector: How Political

Advertisers Target You." ProPublica, July 17, 2018. projects. propublica.org/facebook-ads/.

Mezza, Michele. *Algoritmi di libertà: La potenza del calcolo tra dominio e conflitto* (Algorithms of freedom: Computational power between domination and conflict). Rome: Donzelli Editore, 2018.

Montal, Tal, and Zvie Reich. "I, Robot. You, Journalist: Who Is the Author?" *Digital Journalism* 5, no. 7 (2017): 829–49. www.tandfonline.com/doi/abs/10.1080/21670811.2016.1209083?journalCode=rdij20.

Morley, John. "A Blueprint for Better Program Design." LinkedIn, March 27, 2017. www.linkedin.com/pulse/blueprint-better-program-design-john-morley/.

Moses, Lucia. "The Washington Post's Robot Reporter Has Published 850 Articles in the Past Year." Digiday, September 14, 2017. digiday.com/media/washington-posts-robot-reporter-published-500-articles-last-year/.

Muskus, Jeff. "AI Made Incredible Paintings in About Two Weeks." Bloomberg, May 17, 2018. www.bloomberg.com/news/articles/2018–05–17/ai-made-incredible-paintings-in-about-two-weeks.

Myles, Stuart. "Photomation or Fauxtomation? Automation in the Newsroom and the Impact on Editorial Labour—A Case Study." Presented at the Computation + Journalism Symposium, Miami, FL, February 2019.

Naimat, Aman. *The New Artificial Intelligence Market.* Vol. 1. Sebastopol, CA: O'Reilly Media, 2016.

Newman, Nic. *Journalism, Media, and Technology Trends and Predictions*

2019. Oxford: Reuters Institute for the Study of Journalism, 2019. reutersinstitute.politics.ox.ac.uk/sites/default/ files/2019-01/Newman_Predictions_2019_FINAL.pdf.

Newman, Nic, with Richard Fletcher, Antonis Kalogeropoulos, David A. L. Levy, and Rasmus Kleis Nielsen. *Digital News Report 2018*. Oxford: Reuters Institute for the Study of Journalism, 2018. media.digitalnewsreport.org/wp-content/uploads/2018/06/ digital-news-report-2018.pdf?x89475.

Newmark J-School Staff. "Entrepreneurial Journalism Initiative Kicks Off with Five New Courses." CUNY Newmark Graduate School of Journalism, February 14, 2011. www.journalism.cuny. edu/2011/02/entrepreneurial-journalism-certificate-program-opens-for-business/.

Oda, Shoko. "This Media Startup Is Beating the Competition with a Newsroom Run by Robots." Bloomberg, May 27, 2018. www. bloomberg.com/news/articles/2018–05–27/the-airline-geek-trying-to-build-a-media-giant-with-no-reporters.

O'Neil, Cathy. *Weapons of Math Destruction: How Big Data Increases Inequality and Threatens Democracy*. New York: Crown, 2016.

Overview. "What Did Private Security Contractors Do in Iraq?" February 21, 2012. blog.overviewdocs.com/2012/02/21/iraq-security-contractors/.

Owen, Diana. *The State of Technology in Global Newsrooms* (2017 survey). Washington, DC: International Center for Journalists, 2018. www.icfj.org/sites/default/files/2018-04/ ICFJTechSurveyFINAL.pdf.

Pacheco, Inti, and Stephanie Stamm. "GE CEO Letters Decoded: Shrinking

Ambitions and Disappearing Buzzwords." *Wall Street Journal*, March 1, 2019. www.wsj.com/articles/ge-ceo-letters-decoded-shrinking-ambitions-and-disappearing-buzzwords-11551441600.

Peddie, Sandra, and Adam Playford. "Police Misconduct Hidden from Public by Secrecy Law, Weak Oversight." *Newsday*, December 18, 2013. www.newsday.com/long-island/police-misconduct-hidden-from-public-by-secrecy-law-weak-oversight-1.6630092.

Perrin, Andrew. "Americans Are Changing Their Relationship with Facebook." Pew Research Center, September 5, 2018. www.pewresearch.org/fact-tank/2018/09/05/americans-are-changing-their-relationship-with-facebook/.

Perrin, Nicole. "Amazon Is Now the No. 3 Digital Ad Platform in the US." *eMarketer*, September 19, 2018. www.emarketer.com/content/amazon-is-now-the-no-3-digital-ad-platform-in-the-us.

Plattner, Titus, and Didier Orel. "Addressing Micro-Audiences at Scale." Presented at the Computation + Journalism Symposium, Miami, FL, February 2019.

PricewaterhouseCoopers. "Sizing the Prize: What's the Real Value of AI for your Business and How Can You Capitalise?" August 16, 2017. www.pwc.com/gx/en/issues/analytics/assets/pwc-ai-analysis-sizing-the-prize-report.pdf.

Radford, Alec, Jeffrey Wu, Dario Amodei, Daniela Amodei, Jack Clark, Miles Brundage, and Ilya Sutskever. "Better Language Models and Their Implications." *OpenAI Blog*, February 15, 2019. blog.openai.com/better-language-models/.

Radiolab. "Cicada Tracker." WNYC Studios, accessed June 19, 2019. project.wnyc.org/cicadas/.

Reuters. "Reuters News Tracer: Filtering through the Noise of
    Social Media." Reuters Community, May 15, 2017. www.
    reuterscommunity.com/topics/newsroom-of-the-future/reuters-
    news-tracer-filtering-through-the-noise-of-social-media/.

Robbins, Danny, and Carrie Teegardin. "Still Forgiven: An AJC National
    Investigation." *Atlanta Journal-Constitution*, April 26, 2018.
    doctors.ajc.com/.

Roberts, Jeff John. "News Sites That Take on Big Tech Face Legal Peril."
    Fortune, September 27, 2018. fortune.com/2018/09/27/
    facebook-research-censorship/.

Roush, Chris. "AP Biz Editor Gibbs to Oversee News Partnerships." *Talking
    Biz News*, July 21, 2017. talkingbiznews.com/1/ap-biz-editor-
    gibbs-to-oversee-news-partnerships/.

Royal, Cindy. "The Journalist as Programmer: A Case Study of *The
    New York Times* Interactive News Technology Department."
    International Symposium on Online Journalism 2, no. 1 (2012).
    www.isoj.org/wp-content/uploads/2016/10/ISOJ_Journal_V2_
    N1_2012_Spring.pdf.

Slobin, Sarah. "A Computer Watched the Debates. It Thought Clinton Was
    Happy and Trump Was Angry and Quite Sad." *Quartz*, April 19,
    2017. qz.com/810092/a-computer-watched-the-debates-and-
    thought-clinton-happy-trump-angry-sad/.

Sportradar. "AP to Preview Every NBA Game with Automation from
    HERO Sports, Data from Sportradar." January 24, 2019.
    sportradar.us/2019/01/ap-to-preview-every-nba-game-with-
    automation-from-hero-sports-data-from-sportradar/.

Stahnke, Julian, Tom Lazar, Philip Faigle, and Fabian Mohr.

"Stimmungskurven: Wie geht es uns?" (Mood curves: How are we doing?) *Die Zeit*, March 23, 2017. www.zeit.de/ gesellschaft/2017-03/stimmung-wie-geht-es-uns.

Swenson, Kyle. "A Seattle TV Station Aired Doctored Footage of Trump's Oval Office Speech. The Employee Has Been Fired." *Washington Post*, January 11, 2019. www.washingtonpost.com/ nation/2019/01/11/seattle-tv-station-aired-doctored-footage- trumps-oval-office-speech-employee-has-been-fired/?utm_term=. cdb970ea0968.

Thomas, Kathryn. "How the WSJ iOS Team Promotes Cross-Team Collaboration Through OKR-Driven Feature Requests." *Dow Jones Tech*, May 29, 2018. medium.com/dowjones/how-the-wsj- ios-team-promotes-cross-team-collaboration-through-okr-driven- feature-requests-a3f534bcccb.

Thompson, Alex. "Parallel Narratives: Clinton and Trump Supporters Really Don't Listen to Each Other on Twitter." Vice News, December 8, 2016. news.vice.com/en_us/article/d3xamx/journalists-and- trump-voters-live-in-separate-online-bubbles-mit-analysis-shows.

True Anthem. "Success Story: Hearst Television." Accessed June 19, 2019. www.trueanthem.com/hearst-television/.

U.S. Bureau of Labor Statistics. "Newspaper Publishers Lose Over Half Their Employment from January 2001 to September 2016." April 3, 2017. www.bls.gov/opub/ted/2017/newspaper-publishers- lose-over-half-their-employment-from-january-2001-to- september-2016.htm.

Valentino-DeVries, Jennifer. "AARP and Key Senators Urge Companies to End Age Bias in Recruiting on Facebook." ProPublica, January 8,

2018. www.propublica.org/article/aarp-and-key-senators-urge-companies-to-end-age-bias-in-recruiting-on-facebook.

Vicario, Michela del, Antonio Scala, Guido Caldarelli, H. Eugene Stanley, and Walter Quattrociocchi. "Modeling Confirmation Bias and Polarization." *Scientific Reports* 7, no. 1 (2017). doi:10.1038/srep40391.

Voicebot. *U.S. Smart Speaker Consumer Adoption Report 2019.* January 2019. voicebot.ai/smart-speaker-consumer-adoption-report-2019/.

Wall Street Journal. "Voices from a Divided America." October 29, 2018. www.wsj.com/articles/voices-from-a-divided-america-1540822594.

Wang, Shan. "After Years of Testing, the Wall Street Journal Has Built a Paywall That Bends to the Individual Reader." Nieman Lab, February 22, 2018. www.niemanlab.org/2018/02/after-years-of-testing-the-wall-street-journal-has-built-a-paywall-that-bends-to-the-individual-reader/.

Wang, Shan. "The Wall Street Journal Tested Live Push Notifications, with Some Help from the Guardian's Mobile Lab." Nieman Lab, August 4, 2017. www.niemanlab.org/2017/08/the-wall-street-journal-tested-live-push-notifications-with-some-help-from-the-guardians-mobile-lab/.

WashPost PR. "The Washington Post Establishes a Computational Political Journalism R&D Lab to Augment Its Campaign 2020 Coverage." *WashPost PR Blog,* July 24, 2019. www.washingtonpost.com/pr/2019/07/24/washington-post-establishes-computational-political-journalism-rd-lab-augment-its-campaign-coverage/.

WashPost PR. "The Washington Post Experiments with Automated Storytelling to Help Power 2016 Rio Olympics Coverage." *WashPost PR Blog*, August 5, 2016. www.washingtonpost.com/pr/wp/2016/08/05/the-washington-post-experiments-with-automated-storytelling-to-help-power-2016-rio-olympics-coverage/?utm_term=.85060ab27a8d.

WashPostPR. "The Washington Post Launches on Twitch." *WashPost PR Blog*, July 16, 2018. www.washingtonpost.com/pr/wp/2018/07/16/the-washington-post-launches-on-twitch/?utm_term=.959a16de1e2b.

Wei, Sisi. "Creating Games for Journalism." ProPublica, July 11, 2013. www.propublica.org/nerds/creating-games-for-journalism.

Wibbitz. "How Review-Journal Strengthens the Vegas Community Through Powerful Video Storytelling." Accessed June 19, 2019. www.wibbitz.com/resources/review-journal-local-news-video-case-study/.

Willens, Max. "Forbes Is Building More AI Tools for Its Reporters." Digiday, January 3, 2019. digiday.com/media/forbes-built-a-robot-to-pre-write-articles-for-its-contributors/.

Wilson, Kinsey. "Note from Kinsey Wilson: Marc Lavallee to Head Story[X]." New York Times Company, September 7, 2016. www.nytco.com/press/note-from-kinsey-wilson-marc-lavallee-to-head-storyx/.

Xinhua News Agency. "Xinhua Upgrades AI-Based News Production System." June 15, 2018, www.xinhuanet.com/english/2018-06/15/c_137256200.htm.

Xinhua News Agency. "World's First AI News Anchor Makes 'His' China

Debut." November 8, 2018. www.xinhuanet.com/english/2018-11/08/c_137591813.htm.

Yoneshige, Katsuhiro. "About JX PRESS—English." JX Press. Accessed June 19, 2019. jxpress.net/about/about-jx-press/.

Zarracina, Javier. "The Words of Obama's State of the Union Speeches." *Vox*, January 14, 2016. www.vox.com/2016/1/14/10767748/state-of-union-2016-word-count.

Zhou, Youyou. "Analysis of 141 Hours of Cable News Reveals How Mass Killers Are Really Portrayed." *Quartz*, October 14, 2017. qz.com/1099083/analysis-of-141-hours-of-cable-news-reveals-how-mass-killers-are-really-portrayed/.

Zittrain, Jonathan. "The Hidden Costs of Automated Thinking." *New Yorker*, July 23, 2019. www.newwyorker.com/tech/annals-of-technology/the-hidden-costs-of-automated-thinking.

INDEX

INDEX

metadata, 51, 71, 101, 111–112
Microsoft, 66, 80
minimally viable stories,
    130–132, 140, 155
Missouri School of Journalism, 15, 148
MIT Center for Civic Media, 33
MIT Laboratory for Social
    Machines, 34
mobile, 28, 42, 104–105
monetization, 6, 48–50, 154
MSN.com, 45, 81
multimedia, 8, 109, 115

Narrativa, 44
Narrative Science, 87
National Geographic, 151
National Institute for Computer-
    Assisted Reporting (NICAR), 15
National Post, 100
natural language generation, 44, 72,
    82, 83, 86, 87, 89, 94, 98, 132, 138
natural language processing,
    46, 82, 99, 101, 102, 115
NBC Universal, 112
Netflix, 69
New York Post, 140
New York Times, 38, 80, 100, 109, 111,
    122–123, 135, 138, 140, 143, 151
New Yorker, 151
news bots, 25–26, 42–44, 60,
    87, 91, 131, 138, 151
Newsday, 101
newsgathering, 6–7, 21–22,
    28–29, 34, 103, 117
newsroom transformation, 53, 129, 154
NewsTracer, 29
Newswhip, 140
Northwestern University, 122
Norwegian News Agency, 83
NYU Studio 20, 36

objectives and key results
    (OKRs), 144, 147
OpenAI, 68
Oxford University, 47

paywall, 3

personalization, 14, 27, 46, 102
Pew Research Center, 32, 40, 120
platforms, 6, 8, 10–21, 27, 30, 40–43,
    48–51, 93, 103–104, 115, 147, 151
print news, 4, 8, 13, 22, 28, 49
ProPublica, 120, 123–125
prototype, 36, 111, 130
Pulitzer Prize, 36, 117

Quartz, 57, 101, 103, 138, 149

R&D Lab, 137–139
Radio France, 30
reinforcement learning, 64, 75, 80–81
Reuters Institute for the Study
    of Journalism, 7, 24, 104
Reuters News Agency, 29–30, 42, 51
robotics, 116–118
Romford Recorder, 95
Royal, Cindy, 143

San Francisco Chronicle, 101
Seattle Times, 37
sensor journalism, 18–20, 28–29,
    34, 36–37, 40, 116, 165
sentiment analysis, 31–32, 57, 123, 155
Signal, 31
smart machines, 2, 6, 14,
    47, 60–63, 66, 70
smart speakers, 104–107
Snapchat, 49
social media, 6–10, 13, 18–19,
    28–33, 40–42, 46, 48–51, 72,
    137, 140–141, 155, 157
South Florida Sun Sentinel, 36
speech-to-text, 109
Stanford University, 111
start-ups, 2, 10–12, 15, 62, 73,
    139, 144, 147–148, 154
storytelling formats, 42–43
Stray, Jonathan, 101
structured data, 72, 82–84,
    88–89, 106, 151
supervised learning, 34, 75, 79–81

Tamedia, 131
television, 8, 12–13